THE ALLURING PROBLEM

THE ALLURING PROBLEM

An Essay on Irony

D. J. ENRIGHT

Oxford   New York
OXFORD UNIVERSITY PRESS
1986

Oxford University Press, Walton Street, Oxford OX2 6DP

Oxford New York Toronto
Delhi Bombay Calcutta Madras Karachi
Petaling Jaya Singapore Hong Kong Tokyo
Nairobi Dar es Salaam Cape Town
Melbourne Auckland
and associated companies in
Beirut Berlin Ibadan Nicosia

Oxford is a trade mark of Oxford University Press

British Library Cataloguing in Publication Data
Enright, D. J.
The alluring problem: an essay on irony.
1. Irony
I. Title
808   BH301.17
ISBN 0-19-212253-3

Library of Congress Cataloging in Publication Data
Enright, D. J. (Dennis Joseph), 1920–
The alluring problem.
Bibliography: p. 165
Includes index.
1. Irony in literature.   I. Title.
PN56.I65E57   1986   809'.91   86-5167
ISBN 0-19-212253-3

Set by Colset Private Ltd, Singapore.
Printed in Great Britain
at the University Press, Oxford
by David Stanford
Printer to the University

CONTENTS

Definitions? 1

The Unexamined Life Not Worth
    Living: Kierkegaard, Socrates, Pascal 8

Romantic Irony 12

Milosz and the Case Against 20

Situational 26

Anatomy of an Irony 31

Ironic or Not? 36

Or Only Funny and Sad? 48

Ironies Which Aren't 50

What the Bible Tells Us 56

The Fortunes of Faust 63

Shakespearian 68

Swift, Fielding, and Bad Taste 75

Pope, Grass, and Dogs 80

Northanger Abbey and the Double
    Take 83

Hardy Perennial 85

Jamesian 88

Proustian 96

Freud and the Conservation of Energy 102

Politics 107

Censorship 114

Trade Ironies 121

Love and Death 127

Contents

Sarcasm, the Mighty Brought Low, the
Last Laugh   135

Chinese   145

Negative Freedom   149

Must Irony have a Victim? Can It be
Sweet?   152

Conclusion   162

References   165

Index   175

. . . the problem of irony, beyond compare the
most profound and most alluring in the world.

THOMAS MANN, *Bemühungen*

Things puzzling, contrary or ironic
Revivify me like a tonic . . .

VIKRAM SETH, *The Golden Gate*

The proof of the pudding is in the eating.

Proverb

Definitions?

IRONY had always struck me as *alluring*: a way of making statements, not unlike that of poetry, which through the unexpectedness and the avoidance of head-on assertion had a stronger chance of discomposing, if not winning over, the person addressed. The obvious *problem*, once the genuine article had been disentangled from the idle phantasms that arise out of habit, senseless tics of the mind, was to gauge how effective—by dint of jolting, intriguing, or, in its peculiar fashion, amusing—the irony had proved. Amuse someone, so it has been claimed in another connection, and you may well have your way with her or him.

When later in the proceedings I began to read books on the subject, I got the impression that one common though perhaps only temporary characteristic of their authors—besides an undeveloped sense of humour—was an overdeveloped taste for scientific method, or the outward appearance of it.

Of course there were exceptions. In *The Crazy Fabric* (1965) A. E. Dyson keeps his eye on the text and his hands off it. His chosen writers come out all sounding much the same—good, honest, warm-hearted men, decent in a 'natural' way, and consequently unimpressed by official systems of morality and social behaviour or actively hostile to them. At least this proposition is one we can understand, and it contains some truth.

The most notable exceptions to the rule were D. C. Muecke (*The Compass of Irony*, 1969) and Wayne C. Booth (*A Rhetoric of Irony*, 1974). It was they who gave me the most to think about, the worst headaches and, by having opened up territory I was all set to break new ground in, the acutest pain. Muecke is intelligent, feeling, and at home in languages other than English.

1

Booth is learned and funny, a combination hard to resist. His expositions are brilliant, but irony—whose touch must be light—does at times get crushed under the weight of brilliance. Or else—he says of irony that 'perhaps no other form of human communication does so much with such speed and economy'—it is mislaid under sudden decelerations and profusions. The more sophisticated among us are unused to the obvious and, when duty obliges us to take note, we incline to belabour it as a significant discovery.

'Getting to grips with irony seems to have something in common with gathering the mist,' Muecke remarks: 'there is plenty to take hold of if only one could.' Having, all the same, gathered the mist in generous handfuls, he then endeavours to classify it before it leaks away. So, although he too smiles at the undertaking, does Booth; and that his more elaborate taxonomies carry an ironic air doesn't really help the well-disposed reader, any more than do the accompanying diagrams and graphs. (Can the toughest irony survive behind those bars?) Despite the self-cautioning of both critics, irony becomes dehumanized, not because their selections are inhuman, remote, or arcane, but because it emerges as a complicated game with strict rules (even though you cannot hope to formulate them all) and a virtually infinite number of set techniques and procedures. This is the literary theorist's *métier*, and we cannot say him nay, though we can always stop listening. At some peril to ourselves, it may be—we too yearn for classification, for things in their proper place, we fear chaos, we don't (as one unusual classifier wrote) 'want madhouse and the whole thing there'—but a lesser peril than lies in bowing the neck to his yoke. When the subject is literature it is wise to recur to actual life at fairly frequent intervals to check on one's bearings, just as one does the other way round; otherwise, while it may not kill, the letter can maim.

A light-hearted instance of such earthy recurrence is the modest taxonomy which, with Chaucer in prospect, Raymond Preston found growing in an ordinary garden. (1) Simple: you allude to the beauty of the daisies on your neighbour's lawn; (2)

slightly more complex: you casually draw his attention to the untidiness of your own thriving cabbage-patch; (3) in turn you suffer an irony when your potatoes succumb to blight, this being a flouting of the fitness of things as laid down, we shall see, by the *Concise Oxford Dictionary*; (4) the Socratic variety: your neighbour having recommended a certain fertilizer, you ask him innocently why it is that a small dose of it has ruined your tomatoes.

The present book can be distinguished from those mentioned above in that it makes no attempt to do what they have failed to bring off convincingly. Their authors, and some others, have said excellent things, and said them finely, and I shall be making liberal use of them hereafter. A sound principle is, if you can't beat a saying, then borrow it.

*

There is a faint sense of unease about recent books on irony (and most books on irony, it appears, are recent) which has no connection with the legitimate disquiet concerning the 'negative' side of our subject. This unease must stem from the thought that to talk seriously about irony is to lay one's head on the block. The same is true, more obviously, with scholarly books on humour and the categorization and analysis of jokes, an exercise as heavy as frost when the context has to be supplied. The critic's stance is all wrong; the more earnest he is, the more likely to slip on a succession of banana skins. It is not the absurdity of murdering to dissect or breaking butterflies on wheels, for true ironies are the opposite of fragile. The ironic figure of speech, Kierkegaard noted, is 'like a riddle and its solution possessed simultaneously'. Or, like flashes of lightning, ironies are at once powerful and momentary, and exegesis cannot live up to them in either respect.

Then, too, there are those who, once irony has been imputed, expect to observe one long-lasting lightning-flash, the issue of some Duracell of the imagination. A Chaucerian scholar has remarked on the curious assumption that since Chaucer is often ironic in *The Canterbury Tales*, he must always be ironic. True it

3

is that once you gain a reputation for the habit you will barely be able to enter your local baker's and ask for a loaf without getting a stonily suspicious glare. It is akin to 'looking insolent', which, as *Rameau's Nephew* points out, is much worse than actually being it. 'If you have an insolent character, you insult people only from time to time; if you have an insolent face, you insult them all the time.' The writer on irony is in a fair way to being disliked for setting himself up as smarter than other people (primarily his valued readers) whereas in reality not only are his intentions inoffensive but, by virtue of their earnestness, more often than not they deter him from being clever at all.

It isn't surprising that in acknowledging his debt to friends and colleagues the author of a study of the ironic imagination should feel it advisable to state that all irony had been set aside for the moment. The same author—Alan Wilde, in *Horizons of Assent* (1971)—offers a heady account of how irony works:

Thus irony, as the typical form, at all levels, of this century's response to the problematics of an increasingly recessive and dissolving self and an increasingly randomized world, strives, by constantly reconstituting itself, to achieve the simultaneous acceptance and creation of a world that is both indeterminate and, at the same time, available to consciousness.

This conjures up indistinctly some continuous process or closed system, a self-serving mechanism, a phantom state, or indeed an imperspicuously vicious circle. It proposes, or seems to, the fabrication of a world (a whole one?) which, however 'indeterminate' (vague? or unpredictable? or lacking in character? or inconclusive?), is amenable to—to what? Just to being perceived. Irony is more potent, vigorous, and agile than this report appears to suggest, more closely related to objective realities, more *serious*. However, it is unfair to complain about definitions of the doubtfully definable, and the more so when, like the present writer, one has every intention of evading the challenge.

The shortest definition of irony—and the best in that it

embraces the majority of common cases—is Samuel Johnson's: 'A mode of speech of which the meaning is contrary to the words.' A fuller and admirably terse definition is that of the *Concise Oxford Dictionary*:

Expression of one's meaning by language of opposite or different tendency, esp. simulated adoption of another's point of view or laudatory tone for purpose of ridicule; ill-timed or perverse arrival of event or circumstance in itself desirable, as if in mockery of the fitness of things; use of language that has an inner meaning for a privileged audience and an outer meaning for the persons addressed or concerned . . . [f. L f. Gk. *eirōneia* simulated ignorance (*eirōn* dissembler)].

We shall have occasion later to look at perversity of event or circumstance, and at that famous 'fitness of things', a condition we expect others to cherish and are not invariably keen to observe ourselves.

Yet the more elaborate accounts of scholars—the more exclusive because of their elaboration—can tell us something about specific modes, and about that larger phenomenon, the dark sky on which these flashes print their signals. For Alan Wilde irony is typical of the twentieth century, presumably a symptom of some ongoing crisis. Most sorts of crisis have been with us ever since Adam and Eve were turned out of Eden, yet we have a feeling that the present is truly special in this respect, and not just because the present is where we are. We know more these days about what is going on around us (though, mercifully, too much for us to remember all of it clearly), but more, it seems, *is* going on, part of it to do with that ultimate irony whereby in order to safeguard our future we prepare to destroy ourselves.

More profitable than generalized exposition, the weaving of nets to sieve the mist, is the account derived from a particular occasion which, in turn, illuminates the occasion. An instance of this is William Empson's discussion in *Seven Types of Ambiguity* of the casket scene in *The Merchant of Venice*. While remaining formally obedient to the terms of her father's will, Portia arranges for a song to be sung that shall point Bassanio to the leaden casket. Fancy is bred neither in the heart nor in the head but in the eyes, and there it dies. (Moreover, Empson notes, the first three rhyme words, 'bred', 'head' and 'nourishèd', also rhyme with 'lead'.) And Bassanio takes the hint: 'So may the outward shows be least themselves.' The ensuing 'doubt as to Portia's honesty', a very faint one, is matched by a slightly stronger doubt as to Bassanio's affection. He is only marginally superior to the other suitors, and—more frankly than they—he is marrying for money; he needs cash urgently, and his first reference to Portia sums her up as 'a lady richly left'. Empson follows with a passage akin to part of T. S. Eliot's definition of wit* in the essay on Marvell:

Irony in this subdued sense, as a generous scepticism which can believe at once that people are and are not guilty, is a very normal and essential method . . . people, often, cannot have done both of two things, but they must have been in some way prepared to have done either.

This is the type of irony that doesn't reject or refute or turn upside-down, but quietly casts decent doubt and leaves the question open: not evasiveness or lack of courage or conviction, but an admission that there are times when we cannot be sure, not so much because we don't know enough as because uncertainty is intrinsic, of the essence.

*

Rather than theory, it is something resembling 'practical criticism' that this book will concern itself with: the exploration of individual ironies as they are manifest in life as well as in literature. The lightning-flash—if I may persist in a metaphor which will very soon have to be repudiated—generally explains itself, but I shall hope to study the aftermath, the way the mind retains the impression, and how the landscape is transformed, often for

---

*'It is not cynicism, though it has a kind of toughness which may be confused with cynicism by the tender-minded . . . it is confused with cynicism because it implies a constant inspection and criticism of experience. It involves, probably, a recognition, implicit in the expression of every experience, of other kinds of experience which are possible.'

more than a moment. It is generally granted that irony is devious, yet rarely do we give it the sustained attention—attention to its nuances, its multiple workings, its successive and various effects —which we devote to the most static of poetic images. In fact we think of irony too literally in terms of lightning: either it strikes (preferably somebody else) or it doesn't, but either way it is ephemeral, to be dismissed from consciousness once the danger or the fun is past. We allow it too short a lease, as if it were no more than the little joke that conventionally precedes serious and formal deliberations, or seeks to terminate them.

Erich Heller, who has produced the best non-definitions of it, considers that every assertion ever made of irony, except in its slackest apparitions as a mere mannerism, is such that anyone might legitimately reply: 'Ah, but that is not irony!' Implied in that comment must be my defence of much that follows, together with the mitigating plea that the more time you spend with a subject the less sure you are of where it begins and where it finishes.

Irony . . . irony . . . irony. And we haven't yet started. It is unfortunate, it is even ironical, that for so ubiquitous and multifarious and, some say, alluring a phenomenon there should be but one word.

The Unexamined Life Not Worth Living:
Kierkegaard, Socrates, Pascal

THE long first chapter of Kierkegaard's *The Concept of Irony*, entitled 'The Conception Made Possible', renders the conception virtually impossible to understand. A learned reader of the London Library's copy of the book—learned, to judge from other comments in the same hand—has written on the title-page, 'What is the point?' This reaction and the fact that other men of learning have thought the work to be ambiguous, and conceivably ironic throughout, leaves me less ashamed to admit that a good deal of it is beyond my comprehension.

There are fine and marvellously intelligible passages in it; and unmistakably playful moments too. Hegel saw the ironist as unable to act a proper man's part in the world, being formed of negation and nostalgia, contemptuous of the finite (and of the infinite too?), indulging himself in the bliss of self-enjoyment, enhanced by the annihilation of whatever is noble and great. In short, as the antithesis of the tragic hero, who faces adversity single-mindedly and remains true to himself.* When, in *Vorlesungen über die Aesthetik*, Hegel writes of the ironist that 'Whoever has reached such a standpoint of godlike genius consequently looks down in superior fashion on all other mortals', Kierkegaard observes that, all the same, the great philosopher is himself being ironic in his frequent use of the word 'superior' (*vornehm*) in referring to such people.

'If one must warn against irony as a seducer, one must also

*On this topic see Charles I. Glicksberg, *The Ironic Vision in Modern Literature*, 1969.

8

praise it as a guide' and acknowledge its function as a 'disciplinarian'. There is much in every personal life—says the young Kierkegaard in his academic dissertation—which, like wild shoots, must be pruned away, and 'irony is an excellent surgeon'. He goes further: for as no true philosophy is possible without doubt, so (or so one may claim) no authentic human life is possible without irony. Indeed, it might seem that irony is a cure for all moral ills, in that it 'limits, renders finite, defines, and thereby yields truth, actuality, and content', and moreover 'chastens and punishes and thereby imparts stability, character, and consistency'. Some doubts as to the young scholar's tone—his examiners were not too happy with him—may intervene here, as also during his explanation that, when an ironic figure of speech is misunderstood, it is not the fault of the speaker 'except insofar as he has taken up with such an underhanded patron as irony which is as fond of playing pranks on its friends as its enemies'. Even so, he penetrates to the heart of irony in submitting that, when mastered (i.e. not merely employed in passing or casually), it 'actualizes actuality': which is to say, it dispels illusion, hypocrisy, and deceit, and brings the reality of a situation into focus.

*

The subtitle of Kierkegaard's book is 'With Constant Reference to Socrates'. Socrates introduced irony into the world. He pretended to be ignorant—'Come now, my dear Euthyphro, inform me, that I may be made wiser'—and, under the guise of seeking to be taught by others, he taught others. He asserted that he 'was never anyone's teacher . . . I ask questions, and whoever wishes may answer and hear what I say'; but, in addition to the disclaimer occurring in his *Apology*, one can never repose full trust in the word of an ironist.

The charge against Socrates, according to his own report, had it that he was a busybody, 'investigating the things beneath the earth and in the heavens and'—can this be another definition of irony?—'making the weaker arguments stronger'. And then encouraging others to do likewise. (In the *Euthyphro* he had surmised that the Athenians weren't particularly worried about a man being clever so long as he didn't impart his cleverness to others.) Found guilty, he was allowed to propose an alternative punishment to death. He couldn't opt for a fine since he lacked the wherewithal to pay it, nor would he choose banishment, for if the Athenians weren't able to endure his conversation, who would be? He insisted that he did not deserve an evil fate, which cut out both imprisonment and keeping his mouth closed. So only death remained, for he did not know whether it was an evil or a good.

A further irony which Kierkegaard touches on is that we do not hear Socrates, we hear only the discordant versions of different disciples. He is and he is not, somewhat like Rilke's unicorn; he functions in world history like a dash (Danish: *Tankestreg*, 'thought mark') in punctuation; he is 'the nothingness from which a beginning must be made'. Rather more pointed is Socrates' own worldly-wise irony: those eager to cast a slur on the State will blame the men of Athens for killing him, killing a wise man, 'for,' he warns them disinterestedly, 'you know, those who wish to revile you will say I am wise, even though I am not'.

*

'Socratic irony' is employed by Pascal in his *Provincial Letters* (1656-7) where he plays the well-meaning layman, hungry for enlightenment, asking innocent questions and expressing naïve astonishment at the answers. Illustrations are hard to furnish because of the historical and theological clarification they now require, but Letter VII is something of an exception. The Jesuit Father is unfolding the doctrinal distinction between killing someone *secretly* and killing someone *treacherously*. 'It may be called killing treacherously, when a man slays another who had no reason to expect it. Hence he who slays an enemy cannot be said to kill him treacherously, even if he perpetrates the deed by lying in wait or stabbing him in the back.' It is exactly the same if he slays him after a reconciliation, after giving his word that he will make no attempt on the man's life, just as long as no very close friendship exists or has come to exist between the two of them. The 'pupil' admits that this is a revelation to him—adding that it would seem totally impossible ever to kill a man *treacherously*, since surely no one ever thought of destroying anybody except an enemy. (Pascal had never lived in the inner cities.)

When the discussion moves to the question of killing 'with a good conscience' for slander or the making of contemptuous gestures, the Father states that the Society has ruled that this should not be practised too casually, on petty occasions, and for an obvious reason . . . Yes, his questioner interjects, he knows the reason—because the law of God forbids murder. Not at all, the Father retorts, the reason is that if people were permitted to kill one another merely for name-calling or nose-thumbing, then whole kingdoms would be depopulated, and this would constitute an injury to the State, the which is impermissible.

In the following letter our innocent learns that while it is wrong for a judge to retain money given him by someone in whose favour he has subsequently pronounced a just verdict, he can rightfully keep what he has received from a man in whose favour he has pronounced unjustly. 'Are you not aware that a judge owes *justice* to all, and therefore cannot sell it? But he does not owe *injustice*, and therefore he may sell that.' We are not so remote here from Swift and his *Modest Proposal*.

But the best known of Pascal's ironies, to be taken to heart by all who set pen to paper, comes towards the end of Letter XVI, when he explains apologetically that the letter is longer than usual only because he didn't have the time to make it shorter.

11

Romantic Irony

IT is a long jump from the classical (Socratic irony is distinctly unromantic) to the romantic, and only fear of cowardliness accounts for the presence of this pseudo-chapter. I find the theory of romantic irony hard to grasp and its relevance in practice (i.e. to anything outside itself) even harder to perceive.

Ascribed in its origins, justly or not, to Friedrich Schlegel at the turn of the eighteenth century, in recent years the theory has proved of considerable fodder-value to literary critics no doubt more advanced than he but less serious-minded. Schlegel was something of a philosopher in the old sense.*

Romantische Ironie, it seems, views the world as chaotic, unpredictable, and inexhaustibly fertile, and the artist, in the face of it, as obliged to recognize the limitations of his own consciousness; his perceptions of the infinite are inevitably partial and thus in some degree false, yet he must rightly value them (what else does he have?), and so he preserves a balance in his work between rhapsodic affirmation and sceptical reservation. According to Muecke's conflation, which sounds rather like a vignette from *The Dunciad* or *Absalom and Achitophel*, the romantic ironist

---

*Italo Svevo opined that artists are inspired by philosophers they don't fully understand and in turn philosophers don't understand the artists they inspire; he quoted the story of Wagner sending his music to Schopenhauer, whom he gratefully acknowledged as his master: Schopenhauer wrote back to say that the composer who best reflected his philosophy was Rossini. Nietzsche wrote in a letter to Georg Brandes, 'We philosophers like to be mistaken for artists'; and many artists (queasy word) feel slighted unless someone sees a bit of the philosopher in them. It was Friedrich Schlegel who commented that in the Philosophy of Art one of two things was generally lacking: either philosophy or art.

will be a bundle of paradoxes, 'consciously subjective, enthusiastically rational, and critically emotional'.

In *English Romantic Irony* (1980) Anne K. Mellor does her best and bravest to explain the phenomenon, which she considers 'radically new' around 1800 and related to the various revolutions of the late eighteenth century, political and industrial, and the decline of belief in a neatly God-ordained universe, and then to demonstrate its presence in English writing. She defines the romantic ironist as one

who perceives the universe as an infinitely abundant chaos; who sees his own consciousness as simultaneously limited and involved in a process of growing or becoming; who therefore enthusiastically engages in the difficult but exhilarating balancing between self-creation and self-destruction; and who then articulates this experience in a form that simultaneously creates and de-creates itself . . .

We had better rid our minds of the ingenuous supposition that romantic irony is either romantic or ironic in any generally understood sense of the words. The trouble is that so few seizable defining examples of it are forthcoming.* What can it be of which Byron is the 'most masterful' exponent and which is 'quintessential' in Keats? Which is manifest in *Sartor Resartus*, 'masterfully embodying' an attack on the limits of language (ironically, a favourite pursuit of professional users of language today), and present, if guiltily denied, in Coleridge, and also, though he went in fear of flux and disorder, in Lewis Carroll? Byron, Miss Mellor says, exhibits 'a heroic balancing between enthusiastic commitment and sophisticated scepticism'. Agreed, he is romantic and unromantic, solemn and flippant, high-flown and down-to-earth, by turn.

*The clearest account I have come across, description plus prime example, occurs elsewhere, in Peter Conrad's *Shandyism: The Character of Romantic Irony* (1978): 'Vacillating in this way between prophetic self-assertion and empathetic self-effacement, the romantic poet is necessarily an ironist, flickering like Hamlet between the imperial scope of the mind and its comic condemnation to the prison of the body.' The 'terminal gods' in this 'double plot', he suggests later, are Ariel and Caliban.

13

Well—well, the world must turn upon its axis,
    And all mankind turn with it, heads or tails,
And live, and die, make love, and pay our taxes . . .

The wind swept down the Euxine, and the wave
    Broke foaming o'er the blue Symplegades;
'Tis a grand sight, from off 'the Giant's Grave',
    To watch the progress of those rolling seas
Between the Bosphorus, as they lash and lave
    Europe and Asia, you being quite at ease:
There's not a sea the passenger e'er pukes in,
Turns up more dangerous breakers than the Euxine . . .

Their union was a model to behold,
Serene and noble—conjugal, but cold . . .

Most of us are, in our more modest ways, divided souls. Perhaps
'romantic irony' is simply having it both ways—infinity/
finiteness, angel/ape, passion/reason, power/impotence, praise/
lament, all those ancient dichotomies—on a grander than usual
scale. In which case it is a question of degree, not of kind, and
hence in no need of special treatment. Goethe may have summed
up the topic in his lucid verse epigram: 'If you wish to advance
into the infinite, just follow the finite in all directions.'

Keats mixed ardour with reasoned scepticism; he found life
both beautiful and painful. ('Love in a hut, with water and a
crust, / Is—Love, forgive us!—cinders, ashes, dust' was as near
as he came to Byron, and he soon sheered away.) There is nothing
extraordinary there, nothing unprecedented, apart from the
intensity of Keats's sensations, more justly his ability to persuade
us that what happens is happening for the first time ever. No
doubt 'The Eve of St Agnes' is ambiguous, intentionally or not.
Miss Mellor is as sure that Porphyro takes Madeline's virginity as
if she were on the spot. (What a pity she wasn't present at the
Marabar caves.) This is fine, it suits her book, since romantic love
is seen coexisting with cynical sex, or (in up-to-date terms)
creating and de-creating are going on simultaneously. Surely
what irony there is in or about Keats was characterized by F. R.
Leavis fifty years ago, without the benefit of either jargon or

private-eyeing, when he showed how the 'Ode to a Nightingale' 'moves outwards and upwards towards life as strongly as it moves downwards towards extinction'.

Schlegel declared that irony was nothing to joke about. That's true, of course; and, of course, it isn't true . . . Affirm and deny in one sentence, and you too can be a romantic ironist.

*

Lilian R. Furst is made of sterner stuff, albeit the physical weight of her book, *Fictions of Romantic Irony in European Narrative, 1760–1857* (1984), is at odds with the ethereal abstractions within it. She opens by declaring that 'we must come to grips with irony, and with romantic irony too, if we are to understand modern literature'. It could as well be said that we must come to grips with modern literature if we are to understand irony—though personally I would leave out the word 'modern'. One seems to have encountered similar assertions before, with irony replaced by the Doppelgänger, the Mask, Libido, the Yin and the Yang, Time and Space, the Internal Combustion Engine, or whatever else the writer had picked as his *raison d'écrire*.

If Schlegel didn't invent romantic irony, he made it an eminently respectable research topic by giving it 'a wholly new metaphysical status' and investing it with 'an epistemological and ontological function'. Miss Furst's description of the 'commanding position' thus awarded it smacks of a NASA hand-out:

The dialectic of its tensions is to permeate every facet of the aesthetic artefact, shaping its outer and inner configuration, and this dynamic is to act as the propellant for the advance towards transcendence. The destructive de-creation of irony is envisaged as a vital step for the subsequent re-creation on a higher plane.

But she is at her best with Byron, whose 'inversion of the Don Juan figure from the customary erotomanic predator into an ignorant, immaculate youth "of saintly breeding" ', she observes, corresponds to Johnson's simple concept of irony as reversal.

15

It is specifically romantic irony that makes Byron 'see through the various pretences of the world to the core of doubt' and then enables him to 'transmute the nihilism into something like Friedrich Schlegel's "transzendentale Buffonerie". . . Doubt undermines whatever is written, but even in the process of destruction it leaves space for further buoyant reconstruction.' This scenario explains why *Don Juan* can resemble a perpetual motion machine, promotion followed by demotion, sweetness by sourness, romance by reduction, until the succession of cant-subverting stanzas and cantos grows as wearisome as a sojourn on a see-saw.

Miss Furst does not lack for courage, and is ready to tackle such humble but tricky questions as the difference between irony and satire. The satirist is harsher, employing ridicule, contempt, indignation, anger; his attack is 'grounded in ethical standards', he is a moralist. The ironist, on the other hand, is 'governed by relativities', and doesn't set himself up 'in the authoritative pre-eminence of the judge'. He is not *certain* enough, and 'tends to admit the good *and* the bad in every alternative'. Hence, she concludes, while satire is ostensibly the harsher of the two, it is also the more buoyant since it implies an underlying faith in the potentiality for betterment. 'A pessimistic satirist without that faith would not bother to make his attack.' By contrast, the art of irony, ostensibly less abrasive, may be the more disturbing because it is 'an enquiring mode that exploits discrepancies, challenges assumptions and reflects equivocations' but doesn't presume to hold out answers.

It is meant as a tribute to Miss Furst's exposition to suggest that the considerable light it throws doesn't always fall where intended. To pick holes isn't difficult. The ironist's relativities can be absolutes in light disguise. Satire oftens preaches to the converted; or is buoyed up solely by itself. Both satire and irony may derive from and provide a measure of solace for the pessimist. The satirist isn't always hopeful, and may be short on morality; the ironist isn't always hopeless, and may qualify as a moralist. It all depends. By dint of polarizing, Miss Furst has pinned down a form of satire which isn't irony and a form of irony which isn't satire.*

She adds that the distinction between the two modes is more enigmatic in practice than in theory, adducing the example of Swift on the shakiness of attempting a radical divorce between them. That she retains some faith in the distinction causes her to worry over her summary of irony's 'commanding position', and the sentence about 're-creation on a higher plane', which belongs rather to her account of satire. Hence she warns, 'Instead of ascending into an ecstatic self-liberation, irony may provoke a descent into an agonizing awareness of uncertainty.' She is alive to all the traps and pitfalls—except perhaps one: the incongruity of presenting irony as a solemn and philosophical vision, or something that simultaneously exists everywhere but lives, moves and has its being in the minds of scholars. Her closing sentences ring out like a tocsin:

In the transition from traditional irony to romantic irony, irony within the framework of the fiction is transmuted into an irony of the fiction which may then be potentiated into an irony of fictional irony—and of the fictionality of existence. It is a process that starts with ambiguity, edges from ambivalence to paradox, and ends in an alienating derangement of the text and of the world.

Or rather, I should have said, like a leper's clapper. Irony is plainly something to be avoided.

*

More should be said of Friedrich Schlegel. It was from *Roman*, the word for novel, that he took his adjective *romantisch*; novels, he maintained, are 'the Socratic dialogues of our time'. Romantic poetry, like the perfect novel, was progressive and universal, always in the state of becoming and never to be finished. His own

*A practical way of bringing out the difference between irony and satire with some clarity, August Closs proposes in a letter, is to compare and contrast Thomas Mann and his brother Heinrich.

novel, *Lucinde*, was never finished. On its publication in 1799, and for long thereafter, it was considered nakedly sensual, indecent, a 'dirty book'. Kierkegaard accused it of attempting to eliminate all morality. (Schlegel wrote in his notebooks that 'Morality without a sense for paradox is vulgar.') And its latest translator, Peter Firchow, reports that a recent German edition was illustrated with woodcuts of 'nude figures in various positions' having precious little to do with the text.

The story of—or essay on—the metaphysical/physical relationship between a husband and a wife, both of them fervidly intellectual/artistic and passionately loving, is by modern standards, and by most ancient ones too, a mild affair. It is doubtful whether its high-flown male appreciation of womanhood would find favour with the more irascible class of feminist, but the majority of readers must surely be amused by Schlegel's 'romantic irony' (manifest in the author's interventions *à la* Sterne, for instance in wondering what impression his 'mad little book' will make on various categories of possible readers), and grateful for the momentary eruptions of eroticism amid so much spirituality. An earlier English version (1913) thought fit to omit certain passages in the interests of delicacy and to bowdlerize others. In a comical scene—which none the less, by its indirection, carries quite a charge these days—Julius is on the point of making love to his wife. Lucinde is enticingly coy—'Oh no, Julius! Don't, I beg you; I don't want to'—and he asks, 'Can't I feel if you're as passionate as I am? Oh, at least let me listen to the beating of your heart . . .' This request was watered down to 'May I not feel* * *'—which, ironically, sounds far more indelicate.

'Irony is duty': so spoke Schlegel. But not duty alone induces me to reproduce a passage from a section called 'Of the Nature of Friendship', a fragment of the proposed continuation of *Lucinde*. A joke can joke about anything, Julius tells his friend Lorenzo, a joke is free and universal, but there are places in his being where a joke just isn't bearable. 'It's irony that has often disturbed me in the music of friendship with its distinctly discordant note.'

Lorenzo. So the note was probably put in too often, or in the wrong place. But that's not the fault of the note. Still, you may be right. And who knows if that isn't the irony of irony, that in the end one grows to dislike it.

Julius. The final irony, I think, is to be found rather in that it seems to be becoming impossible for you to talk about irony without being ironic.

Lor. I'm afraid that it's exactly the other way around. Where's the irony, when in bitter earnest one doesn't know where one's at? And the more I think about it, the more incomprehensible it becomes.

Jul. What's the name of the riddle?

Lor. That of all things you should find friendship incompatible with irony.

Jul. Well?

Lor. Well, if irony isn't the real essence of friendship, then perhaps the gods know what it really is, or irony itself knows. I don't.

Jul. And irony does know when its essence is in harmony with its purpose.

Lor. That is, when the friends know it.

Jul. No. They often don't know, but irony does.

Lor. How do you know that, my friend?

Jul. When I myself still wasn't aware, and didn't imagine what this divine quality and struggle in me was, irony already knew where it was tending to and to what end—and irony showed by its actions that it knew. It attached itself profoundly only to what was just and, after a brief experiment, despised all that was unjust; it affirmed itself, expanded, became clear and conscious of its power, became wise, just as everything that is human becomes wise, through action. For surely you don't want to restrict knowledge to everything that can be said.

This is at least preferable to all that talk about 'infinitely teeming chaos' and 'eternal agility'. We might long for a firmer grip on what Julius is saying, but Kierkegaard noted in his journals that the ironical individual cannot be understood by anyone who is full of longing since the latter is always thinking: if only one could have one's wish! Moreover, one wouldn't wish to be one of those who would restrict knowledge to what can actually be said.

19

Milosz and the Case Against

Where irony is not a direct and classic device of oratory, not for a moment equivocal to a healthy mind, it makes for depravity, it becomes a drawback to civilization, an unclean traffic with the forces of reaction, vice, and materialism.

SETTEMBRINI of *The Magic Mountain* is a decent fellow, progressive and humanistic, and given to stating a point of view uncompromisingly and in starkly simple terms. For this, like his 'pupil' Hans Castorp, we are grateful, embracing his pronouncements with our reason, if not with our sympathies. Like Castorp, we ask ourselves: 'Irony that is "not for a moment equivocal"—what kind of irony would that be?' But Settembrini is no mere figure of fun or sciamachic man of straw. Irony doesn't have to be what he says, but it can be found in the disreputable company he shudders over.

In his 1965 preface to the anthology, *Post-War Polish Poetry*, Czeslaw Milosz remarked that for better or for worse irony 'is an ingredient of modern poetry everywhere and cannot be separated from the purpose it serves. As for this purpose, elegant scepticism and the will to defend the basic values of man's existence are not one and the same thing.' In the preface to a later edition (1968) he was more outspoken:

Yes, I know that man uses irony to cope with evil. He throws his defiance to the evil powers of this world in the name of his frail and helpless values. We should not forget, however, that irony is an ambivalent and sometimes dangerous weapon, often corroding the hand which wields it. From what is a desperate protest masked with a smile to nihilistic acquiescence is but one step.

Irony can afford the only possible victory in the face of defeat, a 'moral victory' in the line of Pascal's saying—that man is only a reed, the weakest thing in nature, but he is a thinking reed. The universe, or accident, or disease, may get the better of him, but whereas he knows this, the universe, the accident, the disease, know nothing of it. The snag is that a disposition towards irony, though it may not invite defeat, accepts it too readily. In *The Witness of Poetry* (1983) Milosz asks whether 'the melancholy tone of today's poetry will not be recognized at some point as the veneer of a certain mandatory style', since 'a vision deprived of hope may often be just a cliché common to the poetry of our time'. He allows that if we examine pessimism we cannot guarantee a happy outcome, for we may have to admit that in part at least it is justified.

This 'mandatory style', it is true, can operate as a permanent medical certificate excusing us from active service. Milosz is carrying Hegel's censure a little further, as in our time we would expect. To be vanquished by insurmountable odds, by what is literally irresistible, is no disgrace to an individual. To hand the whole world over to defeat, to capitulation, is a different matter. Yet nihilism, I would think, is a philosophy (a word, if you think of its etymology, too often profaned) which, being not only extreme but extremely presumptuous, is more likely to find a natural enemy in irony than a friend.

Ironically, Milosz could find support in an unwelcome quarter —from one of the revolutionaries in Conrad's *Under Western Eyes*. Sophia Antonovna warns: 'Remember, Razumov, that women, children, and revolutionists hate irony, which is the negation of all saving instincts, of all faith, of all devotion, of all actions.'

Milosz's true enemy is 'the absurd', a still fashionable and increasingly flaccid engagement to show that since all is meaningless, meaninglessness has taken on a meaning. It appears to be practitioners of this cult or something like it (though he calls it 'a mutation in culture') that Lionel Trilling is conscientiously soft on in his essay of 1963, 'The Fate of Pleasure'. Having quoted

Wordsworth's resounding affirmation concerning 'the grand elementary principle of pleasure', that 'native and naked dignity of man', Trilling discusses the 'modern spirituality' which, through violence and through insistence on the sordid and disgusting, seeks to destroy 'specious good'—and pleasure along with it.

Trilling admits that this spirituality cannot be immune to irony, especially since it has invaded popular entertainment. 'How can irony be withheld from an accredited subversiveness, an established moral radicalism, a respectable violence?' That is nicely said. He adds, however, that a merely adversary response, whether irony or something weightier (what? proscription?), will not prove adequate because it leaves out of account 'those psychic energies which press beyond the pleasure principle and even deny it', phenomena which obviously cannot be 'summoned up in felicity' and are 'a means of self-definition and self-affirmation'.

This is to sell irony sadly short: it isn't going to be paralysed or thrown into disarray by words like 'mutation' and 'culture', or even that grim-sounding pleasure principle. Trilling doesn't question those shibboleths, 'self-definition' and 'self-affirmation'; he grants them by default a sort of substantiality, a self-evident virtue, denied to that antique and comical expression 'felicity', clearly something to absent oneself from for more than a while. But what is 'self-definition' likely to be, in this unpleasurable context, except Mohican hair-dos, black leather, and Nazi insignia (de-defining agents though one might have reckoned them),* shading into egotism, incivility, disregard of other people's feelings? And what can 'self-affirmation' be in effect, except the same plus mugging and rape, rioting in football grounds, and burning down the dwellings of people whose race or colour you don't like? Incidentally, some of these defining activities have flourished during a period when there was no strong, central, strait-jacketing authority to react or rebel

*Thus Elaine Dundy, in *The Dud Avocado* (1958), of Americans in Paris: 'A rowdy bunch on the whole, they were most of them so violently individualistic as to be practically interchangeable.'

against. By contrast, demonstrators in Warsaw in the early 1980s
were dressed like shabby but decent artisans, respectable clerks,
churchwardens and small shopkeepers. The effect was one of
greater authenticity.

As for those 'psychic energies', we know that they exist in
forms more felicitous than the ones I have touched on; we also
know that we have to try to contain them in some of their mani-
festations, not at any rate to make entertainment out of them.
(Or if we do, let's not call it literature.) What Trilling treats with
kid-glove respect is a 'mandatory style' rather than anything so
grand as a mutation, a once good cause which came to gratify
what Wordsworth in that same *Preface* termed a 'degrading
thirst after outrageous stimulation', and hence—with the help in
intellectual circles of the anticipated though *après-nous* End of
the World—has proved relatively long-lived. Old causes can turn
into new mischiefs. How refreshing it is these days to meet a
contentedly undefined, a peacefully unaffirmed self!

*

It may be that his understandable animus against clichés of
despondency has rendered Milosz incautious on occasion.

> Human reason is beautiful and invincible . . .
> Is an enemy of despair and a friend of hope . . .
> Beautiful and very young are Philo-Sophia
> And poetry, her ally in the service of the good.

These lines from *The Separate Notebooks* (1984) have something
voulu about them; they are vulnerable to even the least malignant
of ironists. But the commemorations and celebrations of that
collection are neither casually expressed nor easily won—'In the
hall of pain, what abundance on the table!'—and I would not
dare, let alone feel obliged, to sneer.

In fact Milosz has used irony in 'Child of Europe' to overturn
the species of 'acquiescing' irony he distrusts:

> Learn to predict a fire with unerring precision.
> Then burn the house down to fulfil the prediction . . .

Love no country: countries soon disappear.
Love no city: cities are soon rubble . . .
Do not love people: people soon perish.
Or they are wronged and call for your help.

And in *The Land of Ulro* (1981) he characterizes the triumph of modern poetry and the various isms of the 1920s and 1930s, whereby a highly obscure and seemingly coterie verse became mainstream, as another prank staged by 'that mistress of irony', History. He relates there the sad history of the Polish ambassador at The Hague who in 1951 received a warning message to the effect that he was about to be charged with some offence against the State: 'Do not return to Warsaw or you'll meet with an accident.' Nevertheless he set out for Warsaw by car, and *en route* was killed in a collision with a lorry. An irony—Milosz doesn't use the word—merely of coincidence, dependent on the locution 'meet with an accident', and not one we would be proud of adducing.

'From Mythology', a prose poem by his younger compatriot Zbigniew Herbert, which Milosz himself translated into English, remains ambiguous. First there was a savage god, then there were the family gods of the republic, a bourgeois lot with their harmless thunderbolts. Eventually 'only superstitious neurotics carried in their pockets little statues of salt representing the god of irony. There was no greater god at that time.' The story ends with the coming of the barbarians: 'They too valued highly the little god of irony. They would crush it under their heels and add it to their dishes.' Possibly Herbert, and we, are to be numbered among those superstitious neurotics: irony couldn't have achieved much, but no greater god was available. We cannot believe that barbarians would prize irony—though they may have appreciated its value as a highbrow equivalent of bread and circuses—but, being blessed with a healthy appetite, they might well discover the uses of salt: the metaphorical 'ironically', i.e. aptly, declining into the literal. If we suppose there is an allusion to Matthew 5: 13, the salt must have lost its savour and was only good to be trodden underfoot—which would suggest that in their breezy undiscriminating way the barbarians took whatever they came upon in their stride, and regarded those surviving neurotics with derision. The metaphor is an old one; Goethe described irony as 'the little grain of salt which alone renders the dish relishable'.

*

The case against irony has of course been made regularly throughout the centuries. Henri Frédéric Amiel referred to it variously as frivolous, supercilious, egotistical, malicious, and bowelless, while a character in Heinrich Böll's *Billiards at Half-past Nine* (1962) spoke of 'keeping your superiority feelings fresh in a refrigerator of irony'. In *Metahistory: The Historical Imagination in Nineteenth-Century Europe* (1974), Hayden White declares that in its apprehension of the folly or absurdity of the human condition, irony encourages a belief in the 'madness' of civilization and tends to inspire 'a Mandarin-like disdain for those seeking to grasp the nature of social reality in either science or art'. It must require a peculiarly monolithic, brutish and deadening exercise in irony to do all that! Why, in *Doctor Faustus* we hear that 'there is true passion only in the ambiguous and ironic'. Admittedly, it is the Devil speaking, or so we are led to believe, and he has an axe to grind. But that doesn't mean that, whatever spirit he spoke in, what he said wasn't meant to be taken as true, or true to a degree, or at times, or in places.

It was all very well for Ortega y Gasset, in *The Dehumanization of Art*, to doubt that any young person of the time could be impressed by a poem or a painting or a piece of music that was not flavoured with a dash of irony. That was in 1925, since when much has happened. No one would wish for ironic pleasures in, say, Jaroslav Seifert's late, retrospective love poetry. 'What more beautiful gift has life to give / than love?' This is what—among other things—his Czech public want, need, and deserve: direct, unequivocal human warmth, a celebration akin in its simpler way to Milosz's.

*

Possibly the question isn't quite as contorted as all this has made out. Talking of Corbière, in 1912 the Frenchman Charles Morice distinguished between two classes of irony: the affirmative, which proceeds from 'love and its laughter', and the negative, 'a grimace of impotence', which is incapable of enduring a powerful thought or a heroic gesture, detests nature, wears a mechanical grin over its forced gaiety, and in short is 'the pestilential product of the boulevard'. That sounds straightforward enough. Yet we perceive that the negative type is easier to locate and map, to wax eloquent over and to judge, than the affirmative. Does the Devil have all the best tunes, then, or only the most insidious?

I think myself we should take Thomas Mann's Devil with a grain of salt, exactly as we take his antithesis, Settembrini, so much more decent (more so than Sophia Antonovna, too) and so much less clever. An entry in 'Braithwaite's Dictionary of Accepted Ideas', incorporated in Julian Barnes's *Flaubert's Parrot* (1984), judiciously leaves the question open. '*Irony*. The modern mode: either the devil's mark or the snorkel of sanity.'

Situational

NOTHING is spoken by anybody, one uninvolved person is silently contemplating an event or state of affairs which may not even involve anyone else. But it is probably true, or nearly always, that—as Muecke asserts—we shall not view a situation as ironic unless we believe there are those, somewhere or other, who do not. Life, as he says, is forever presenting us with ready-made

26

ironic juxtapositions: 'as when in a bookshelf we find, for example, *Lolita* accidentally alongside *Alice in Wonderland*'. All the same there are, one gathers, those who would place these books together with a sense of exquisite appropriateness, associating the author of the second with the hero of the first. Some surprise was felt by Alfred Appel, Jr., however, when in 1955 he spotted *Lolita* in a Paris bookshop flanked by copies of *Until She Screams* and *The Sexual Life of Robinson Crusoe.* (All three of them published by Olympia Press.) Incidentally, *aficionados* of Nabokov will no doubt produce some irony-proof explanation of why, in a lecture at Cornell University in 1954, when he was completing his novel, he complained of *Ulysses*, according to Appel's class notes, that 'sexual affairs heap indecency upon indecency' and that Leopold Bloom's 'sexual deportment' was 'extremely perverse'. I advance this story merely as an illustration of the elementary pot-lectures-kettle order.

Still on the subject of books: many years ago, when public libraries aimed to encourage borrowings other than of fiction, a friend of mine was prevented from taking out *Murder in the Cathedral* on a non-fiction ticket because it was plainly a thriller. Prone to such misconstructions, the same friend, wishing to buy a recording of Mahler's *Songs on the Deaths of Children*, was after a search offered *Pavane for a Dead Infanta* as a suitable substitute. Could these be cases of incurred irony? On the first occasion, yes: for a librarian ought to know something about books, and this one deserves to be gently mocked. On the second, no: the assistant in the record shop should be praised for making an effort to satisfy a customer, one moreover of shady tastes.

We wonder how conscious of the funny side the Montreal police sergeant was when he told the court that he had been bitten by a nun belonging to a sect called the Apostles of Infinite Love while trying to arrest her for soliciting donations without a permit. This incident was reported in *The Times* of 10 January 1985. Three days earlier the same newspaper carried a letter on the subject of chivalry and the obstacles to it posed by the rules and regulations laid down by local authorities. The writer, 'nudging

80', had given up his seat in a London bus to a lady. At that very moment the conductor descended from the top deck, shouted 'No standing!', and threw him off. The irony belongs to the subsection covering good acts rewarded with ill. (Not quite the same bracket as includes the boy scout who escorted an old lady across a busy street she didn't want to cross.) Good behaviour, consideration, chivalry—but would the gentleman have done as he did had he known what would be done to him? Probably, and with reason, not; we reckon that, while we shouldn't expect to gain from little acts of kindness, we oughtn't to suffer by them either. The perfect gentle knight who would do anything for his lady love quite rightly declined to humour her whim that he should bring her some rubbishy little flower growing half-way down a steep cliff. The seventeenth-century poet William Walsh has a verse sadly but sensibly reflecting

> That a lover forsaken
> A new love may get,
> But a neck when once broken
> Can never be set.

On 13 March 1985 *The Times* carried a report from Peking on how thirteen people were killed while crossing a railway track on their way to a funeral, and another report about a New Yorker suing the estate of a banker's widow who in a suicide leap from the nineteenth floor had landed on him. He contended that the lady jumped 'without regard for human safety'. An equally or more unfunny story—related to me by a friend of the woman in the case—concerns a rapist who broke off to reproach his victim: 'You don't think of anybody's feelings but your own!' It appears that the memory of this remark, its quite peculiar irony, has proved something of a support to her. Perhaps Borges, who 'always imagined Paradise to be a sort of library', has found comfort in identifying the 'magnificent irony' whereby God made him blind.

Life's ironies jostle us in the street. Mrs X hasn't been seen around for some time, normally you spot her out shopping or feeding the birds, practically every day. She's known to have 'a heart condition'. So a neighbour goes to her house to investigate, somewhat reluctantly for this isn't a matey district, we keep our-selves to ourselves. The first snow of winter has fallen, and the neighbour slips and breaks a leg. Later it is established that Mrs X was away visiting a brother in sunny Australia. The incident raised a shamefaced half-smile in the street. It didn't amuse the neighbour at the time, but now she enjoys recounting the story. Though ill rewarded, her intentions do her credit.

We doubt that Nero, for all his weird sense of humour, would have appreciated the joke conveyed in Cavafy's poem, 'Nero's Deadline'. Why should he worry about the Delphic Oracle and its 'Beware the age of seventy-three'? He is only thirty and, even assuming he isn't immortal, has plenty of time to enjoy himself yet. But Galba, preparing an army in Spain and soon to oust him, is in his seventy-third year. More recently, the story goes, a music publisher commissioned a work from Stravinsky, who declined on the grounds that the fee was insultingly small. The same proposal was then made to the indigent Satie, who declined on the grounds that the fee was insultingly large. Satie comes well out of the story, but perhaps wouldn't have recounted it too often since he subsequently swallowed his pride and took the job.

We do not need Thomas Hardy's heavy guns to convince us that life's little ironies don't always work in favour of the good or the good cause. (If they did, they wouldn't be ironies.) Regimes that extort obedience through torture may be fragile, as is said, but before they collapse a lot of people have suffered horribly; and without savouring the irony, noted by Auden, whereby while the martyrdom is in progress, the torturer's horse scratches its 'innocent behind' against a tree. When campaigners for animal rights (since animals don't keep on about their rights, perhaps they should be allowed a few) opened a pheasant enclosure to let the young birds out, the birds preferred to stay inside where it was warm and food was provided. In case this wasn't sufficiently ironic, a fox later entered the enclosure and killed the pheasants. And in 1985 the Royal Society for the Protection of Birds decided to abandon its policy of shaming convicted nest raiders by publishing their names and addresses because the egg thieves were contacting one another with a view to improving their techniques. As it is written, the tabernacles of robbers prosper.

The courteous gentleman on the London bus received what he didn't expect. According to an anecdote Angus Wilson relates in the Royal Society of Literature's *Essays by Divers Hands*, Vol. XLIII (1984), as a young man he once failed to receive what he had expected. At a party given in 1931 after a performance of *The Importance of Being Earnest* at Westminster School, he found himself sitting next to that 'aged Apollo, one of my great romantic heroes', Lord Alfred Douglas. Thrilled, the seventeen-year-old schoolboy, who had just acted Miss Prism, put what he supposed to be the right question: 'Did not Mr Wilde, Sir, believe that Shakespeare's heroines should be acted by boys?' Lord Alfred, clearly irritated, answered, 'Very likely', and then proceeded to give his earnest young interlocutor a list of the winning horses in the races at Lingfield that day.

Authors frequently have occasion to extricate themselves from their reputations or to fend off either innocent questioners or impudent critics. The most devastating reply in these circumstances, and perhaps the most poignant, could be Goethe's, addressed to those who reproved him for indifference to religion. 'I a heathen? After all, I had Gretchen executed and Ottilie starve to death. Isn't that enough for these people? What more do they want?'

Anatomy of an Irony

WE have all heard of the patient who calculates that if he benefits from a dose of three tablets a day, twelve will do him four times as much good. And probably of the young motorcyclist who meets with a nasty accident when riding home after passing the driving test. Also, more cheerfully, of the 'born leader', bossily instructing others in where to put their feet, and falling into a ravine. Then there was the person who lived in a land famous for skilled burglars, and in a tropical-style house open to the elements on all sides, and therefore, as the custom was, acquired an Alsatian dog, and became the only person ever to be bitten by it. (He bit it back, and there was no replay.) It was the same man who, staying overnight with family in the Taj Mahal Hotel, Bombay, sought to save money by eating at a supposedly modest curry place in town rather than in the grandiose hotel restaurant. And discovered the next morning that dinner had been included in the price of the room.

We hear that Dr Guillotin was actually a humane physician who advocated a mode of execution entailing the minimum pain, and then had it named after him despite his protests. It would have been more amusing had he, in a capital variation on the hoist-with-own-petard theme, been bitten by it himself. (The Dr Guillotin who did meet with this fate was a different man.) However, we read in the Book of Esther how Haman was hanged on the gallows, fifty cubits high, he had prepared for Mordecai. And it was an old-style executioner in 1625 who failed in twenty-nine attempts to strike off the condemned man's head, so enraging the spectators, whether by his professional incompetence or the prolonged suffering of the victim, that they stormed the scaffold and killed him with his own axe.

We have seen repeatedly in films the hard-working bank robber whose loot, at the moment of exultation, is scattered by the wind, and we have heard the story of the harder-working countryman who saved up his wages over many years, took a train to the metropolis with the intention of having a jolly good time, and was robbed of everything before he got there. (He redeemed himself by the stoical observation, 'Easy come, easy go.') We know—if only because *Brewer's Dictionary of Phrase and Fable* gives it as a defining example of the irony of fate—that by an irony of fate Joseph became the saviour of the brethren who had cast him into a pit and then sold him to the Midianites. We are aware that, by a more pathetic irony, Molière was on stage playing the title-role in his comedy *Le Malade imaginaire* when he suffered his fatal collapse.

While they have their individual flavour, these particular cases are plain and artless to the point of being transparent. Not all are, by any means. Yet, with the possible exception of those directed at ourselves, ironies are generally so easily recognized as such that we rarely stop to examine them, let alone follow them through. We know an irony when we see one; only he who begins to write about the subject risks sinking into uncertainty and discomfort.

*

In Thailand people can acquire merit in the eyes of Buddha by purchasing trapped birds in the street and releasing them. 'He prayeth best, who loveth best . . .': this would seem more respectable than the old practice of buying indulgences from professional pardoners. However, one popular theory has it that the birds are trained to return to the vendor, who then sells them anew to the next pious passer-by.

Is there irony in this? Yes, if the theory is true and the buyer doesn't know or doesn't believe it. He is then 'the innocent', the butt. He has sought to perform a meritorious act and he has been fooled. Or, a more pungent irony, he was seeking only to do himself a good turn on the cheap, and never mind the poor birds, and he has ended up a few coins the poorer, as he richly deserves. Or—if the theory is untrue—still better, or worse: he has brought about the release of birds who would fare better in captivity since someone further along in the market will snare them and roast them for eating. No merit there.

Even so, there can be nothing deplorable in desiring to acquire merit, for all that this seems an oddly trifling way of going about it. Caged birds usually look unhappy. And the man was sincere, his intentions were good, and in the eyes of Buddha, we take it, intentions do count. That he may have been deceived cannot be held against him. Merit has nothing to do with intelligence.

We may wonder what Buddha will think of the trapper and exploiter of birds. Are demerits noted down? Will he be re-incarnated as a feathered creature, innocent of sin but beset by predators? He may be supporting his family in the only way he can find; he may even be treating the birds well, for they are his unwitting partners in the swindle. If swindle it is. Conceivably the seller will himself acquire merit, either way, or at least avoid a black mark, by being the means whereby someone else acquires merit.

In that case what are we to think of the hypothetical RSPCA inspector, moved by honest indignation, who smashes the cages, finds a good home for the birds, and hauls the offender off to justice? Will he store up spiritual riches for himself, or incur a penalty for interfering in religious affairs? (The fear has been expressed that there is no certain end to the attack on superstition; it is not only the poetry of life, as Goethe claimed, but also the cement of religion.) Merit is altogether a strange business, the gaining of it being often competitive, unseemly though that is. An explanation put forward for the large number of crumbling temples in this part of the world has it that no wealthy man wants to repair a religious edifice built by someone else, whatever its charms, because he wouldn't get the maximum return on his investment, the spiritual interest would be shared with the original builder.

Many different ironies lurk in this matter of the caged birds. Their kind will depend on the circumstances, of which only a few of the more obvious are sketched above. Who, short of Buddha, could possibly have full knowledge of them?

*

Not all the circumstances are known to me in the affair of the man, a Mancunian I believe, who claimed for severe back injuries suffered in an accident. The agent sent by the insurance company to check on him let down a tyre of the claimant's car and photographed him in the act of changing the wheel. Subsequently the court awarded heavy damages against the insurance company. On what grounds? For trespass on private property? For unlawfully letting the air out of a tyre? Or for causing the man to injure his back while changing the wheel? But we are not displeased that the lot of the *agent provocateur* should now and then be an unhappy one.

Not all real-life situations lend themselves so comfortably to speculation and analysis. A story well known to China experts— no doubt because of its emblematic qualities—concerns a poor peasant woman during the civil war of 1945–8. She and her husband lived on the earnings of their only son, a miner. Then, relatively late in life, she gave birth to another son. Normally this would have been a cause for joy; it was not in this case. The elder son, hitherto exempt as an only son, would now be called up for military service, and the parents left destitute. To restore the *status quo ante*, the mother killed the baby. Another irony here: more often this was the fate of *girl* babies.

The woman's emblematic value having ceased, it is not recorded what happened thereafter. The offence of infanticide may have taken second place to the crime of aiding and abetting someone in the evading of his patriotic duty. Possibly she was put to death for committing an act intended to keep her and her husband alive. In which case—assuming that his father had been acquitted of conspiracy—the surviving son would presumably still be excused from serving in whichever army had the upper hand in the region. (But let us leave aside the irony of 'civil' war, and Shakespeare's tableau of the son who unwittingly kills his father and the father who unwittingly kills his son.) At all events, we can be sure that the residual family did not live happily ever after. The mother's dilemma was insoluble; whatever she did she couldn't win. And what she did, she did out of despair, not through cool calculation. (The arithmetic is all mine.) In such situations the detection of an ironic twist is supposed to make us feel better. In this instance it can only make us feel slightly worse.

*

And so to something less grievous, though I could wish it were not necessary to relate the story in the first person singular.

In a reckless moment, with winter approaching and its high bills to follow, I applied to transfer to the heating system known as System Seven and to buy three new and economical storage heaters. I paid on the nail, and the installation was carried out after no more than a month's wait. Then it turned out that the electricians had omitted to change the meter—perhaps it was the job of some different class of electricians—and so no economy was being effected. Also, one of the new heaters was plainly defective, its maximum output rather lower than the others' minimum. There followed phone calls and letters to London Electricity Southern Division, and appointments and promises made and broken. More often than not the switchboard was busy or the operator disinclined to pick up the telephone. On one occasion a man came to the house unannounced and no one was in; more commonly, one was in but no men came. Or they came only to examine the meter and advise that if I wanted it changed I should apply in writing to transfer to System Seven, or to admit cheerfully that for once they happened not to have the right meter on them, or to agree that the heater was indeed defective but I shouldn't worry since it was under guarantee.

Another five weeks went by, several of them exceptionally cold, while I rang other telephone numbers, other divisions, in the hope that they might pass on news of my plight. It seemed that

London Electricity and I just couldn't get together. But on the 24th of February there arrived a handsome St Valentine's card from them featuring a crimson heart set against a doily. Inside I was invited to 'take advantage' of 'warm-heated, adaptable and economical' System Seven and hurry to install it or her. The inscription on the front of the card read: 'IT'S TIME WE GOT TOGETHER!'

A trivial, tedious and commonplace story, I fear, for which the sole excuse is that the glimpse of a hovering irony, however faint, can be the only way to get a little of one's own back on bodies and institutions impregnable to reasoned expostulation.

Ironic or Not?

It is the nature of a hypothesis, when once a man has conceived it, that it assimilates every thing to itself, as proper nourishment; and, from the first moment of your begetting it, it generally grows the stronger by every thing you see, hear, read, or understand. This is of great use.

ANYONE who has propounded a theory or compiled an anthology on a particular theme will appreciate the truth of this passage from *Tristram Shandy*. Everything you happen on is grist to the mill, ripe evidences fall about your head, it all *fits in*. And this is of great use. Later you may suspect that in a prolonged fit of hyperactivity your current preoccupation has cast its colouring on all around, ousting—in your eyes—the true, intrinsic shades of significance. By then it is too late.

*

In *The King's English* the Fowlers make gentle mock of those pessimists who deem it advisable to assist the reader with quotation marks, italics, or question marks inside brackets, as for example Marie Corelli: 'Was I about to discover that the supposed "woman-hater" had been tamed and caught at last?' Even so, I have heard of an English teacher in Japan early this century who issued his students with texts of Dickens carrying a marginal sign for 'humour' (i.e. laugh here), while D. C. Muecke cites the proposal made in 1899 by a certain Alcanter de Brahm for a special convention, a reversed question mark:'ʕ', which he termed 'le petit signe flagellateur', to signal the presence of irony. I wondered whether this passage in Muecke shouldn't itself be accompanied by some sign for humour or hoax, and so perhaps did Wayne C. Booth, since he wrote enquiringly to Muecke on the subject. Reply came that Alcanter de Brahm was real, and really a Marcel Bernhardt, and the book in which the suggestion was made was called *L'Ostensoir des ironies*. A trace of doubt remained in my mind, for writers on irony are hardly more trustworthy than practitioners of it, until I discovered the charmingly entitled work, under Brahm, Alcanter de, in the *Catalogue Général* of the *Bibliothèque Nationale*.

A report on a television interview with 'the pre-eminent articulate rock star of the age', begins thus: 'The trouble with Mick Jagger is that he is insufficiently conscious of his social responsibilities.' How are we to take that statement? The name of the journalist provided me, at any rate, with no clue, and that the paper was *The Times* was no great help. Social responsibility is obviously something important. At the same time, the more often we hear the phrase the more muggings, murders, and child rapes we hear of. Or perhaps we have heard it just too often: the media too are great equivocators, they make and they mar, they persuade us and they dishearten us.

Later Jagger is recorded as hesitating to claim that any of his songs are important: 'That's getting into the pretentious area.' We assume the journalist doesn't approve of pretentious areas: in which case the opening statement is presumably meant ironically, as if to say, a good thing about Mick Jagger is that he doesn't go on self-importantly about his social responsibilities. The suspicion lurks, in my mind at least, that the journalist would have found the writing of the report easier had Jagger come up with a few quotable profundities, pretentious or otherwise, and was consequently a shade loath to praise the suddenly inarticulate rock star unequivocally.

Paul Theroux's comment in an essay, 'The Last Laugh', on S. J. Perelman and his thoughts of settling in England—'He was too much of an Anglophile to like England greatly'—may strike the hasty reader as a staggering, hundred per cent paradox, no less blatant for dodging across linguistic frontiers. But it makes perfect if painful sense. When I lived in Japan in the 1950s I would tremble at the thought of my colleagues, those elderly teachers of English literature, votaries of Johnson and his Age or of Blake and his, actually visiting the England of our age. England, I wanted to say, remembering Henry James's verdict on Tennyson and hoping to spare them 'the full, the monstrous demonstration', is not exactly English.

The *Spectator* of 31 August 1711 contained a letter purportedly written by an ageing gallant in which he complained that in the not so old days you only had to amuse a woman and you could have your way with her, but now the periodical, with its earnest talk of Reason and the Dignity of Human Nature, had arrogantly undermined the very foundations of civilized behaviour. The letter ended: 'In short, Sir, you do not write like a Gentleman.' Steele of course intended this as an irony unconsciously inflicted on himself by the dissolute and foolish correspondent; but by the standards of the gallant—who would agree with an observation in Sheridan's *The Duenna* that conscience has no more to do with gallantry than it has with politics—Steele *was* no gentleman and there was no self-inflicted wound to be seen. All depends on the definition of that shifty word 'gentleman'. A less debatable success, a less transient one since the aesthetes are always with us, is Steele's witticism (9 January 1712), apropos of the Restoration theatre, to the effect that for the critics of the time an insult against all ten of the commandments was less grave than the failure to observe one of the dramatic unities.

It was the failure to observe meaning that distressed Kingsley Amis in the sentence, 'The Americans really have a free Press; it's incarcerated in their constitution', once he had established beyond reasonable doubt that no ironic nuance was intended and the word should have been 'incorporated'. When he adduced another sentence, 'New York City is paranoid—with reason—about rising crime', he probably expected us to feel indignant rather than amused. Yet there could be a nuance there: Montherlant wrote that 'the sad thing about worriers is that they always have reason to be worried'.

*

Real-life incidents can leave us feeling as unsure as do the utterances of thinking reeds. It was announced in May 1985 that crocodile meat for human consumption was about to be available in Australian grocery stores since the reptile was no longer an endangered species. At first sight or sound we might discern an ingredient of paradox if not of irony here, prompted by the consideration that the availability of a species in shops selling foodstuffs implies that the species is in danger of being eaten. But of course it is members of the species (no longer, one imagines, described as 'reptiles') that are destined for the pot, not the species. The latter, we assume, is ensuring its survival thanks to enhanced reproductiveness, this in turn thanks to something else. For all that, individual crocodiles might feel a not altogether logical nostalgia for the days when they belonged to an endangered species and would never see the inside of a butcher's shop.

Another endangered species may have been at the back of the mind of whoever framed a British Rail poster detailing the modes of payment—cheque, credit card, etc.—by which season tickets and the like can be purchased. It concludes, 'Cash is, of course, quite acceptable.' Almost certainly not irony, as one would like to believe, but perhaps indicative of a faint sense that there are still old-world peasants who carry cash on them. The poster, it must be said, is more literate than some. Notices displayed in my local Underground station, famous as the nearest to the Wimbledon Tennis Club, customarily refer to it as 'Sothfilds'. But this may be an Asian transliteration. While in the neighbourhood, I might mention that a car sticker on a car parked near the mosque in Southfields bore the touching device: 'GOD BLESS PAKISTAN and please hurry!' Spotlessly honest and heartfelt, I am sure.

In the late 1950s an American newspaper, the *International Herald Tribune* if I remember correctly, sponsored a competition for essays written by students at Chulalongkorn University in Bangkok. The theme, one of suitably humane import, socially responsible you might say, was 'Is samlor-driving beneath human dignity?' (The samlor, or trishaw, was at that date ubiquitous in Thai cities, and the driver's life was rendered hard by the humpbacked little bridges over the klongs, or canals.) The entrants in the competition turned out to be firmly of one mind: riding in samlors was undeniably beneath human dignity in that passengers could easily be thrown out into the road and run over by cars and lorries, therefore dignity required one to use taxis.

Was the laugh on the essayists, who hadn't for a moment imagined it was the dignity of the samlor-drivers, lowest of the low, that was in question? Or on the sponsors for assuming that the Western concept would be at once comprehensible to a people who combined Buddhist acceptance of earthly hardship with a strong persuasion that the best form of human dignity was self-preservation? The West, mainly in the form of the United States, was at the time keen to keep Marshal Sarit in power, not because of any positive admiration for his behaviour but because he was manifestly anti-Communist; you would not find him worrying about the condition of samlor-drivers and the like. I have to admit to an uneasy feeling that it was I who thought up the topic, though with what design in mind I cannot now say.

The Times of 16 August 1985 touched on two non-verbal ironies, one visual and one auditory. It seems that a painting newly hung above the counter where Liverpool Council members claim expenses is called 'The Cheat'. What the intention was, if any, is not revealed. On another page we read that the opening music for a hard-hitting television documentary on the troubled relationship between doctor and patient was taken from the cheery theme tune of *Doctor Finlay's Casebook*. The latter, possibly the former too, compares well with the ironies of juxtaposition that surrealist painters and writers—Magritte's painting of 'Night Falling' and breaking a window pane, Lautréamont's meeting of a sewing-machine and an umbrella on a dissecting table—rarely brought off at all tellingly.

*

Then there are abbreviations and acronyms, themselves a part of real and often earnest life. As regards the former it must suffice to mention Chesterton's 'Ballad of Abbreviations' and the go-getting American, so busy and pressed for time that

> he yells for what he calls the Elevator,
> A slang abbreviation for a lift.

In the *Listener* of 4 April 1985 Fritz Spiegl listed acronyms which seem to suggest that their makers favour pronounceable words but don't always pay attention to what the words mean. CREEP, Nixon's Committee for the Re-election of the President, was not a great advance on the originally conceived CRAP. Then there are DOG, or Doctors and Overpopulation Group; UNIFIL ('I thought it was some patent cushion-filler,' Mr Spiegl confessed, 'but it turns out to be the UN Force in Lebanon'); AIDS of course (though what is represented is the opposite of what is expressed); and VULVA, Vintners' and United Licensed Victuallers' Association—but no, although he says he read it in the papers, surely Mr Spiegl must be making this one up?*

But what I did read in the papers, more precisely on the back page of *The Times Literary Supplement*, 12 April 1985, was GLIB, standing for Gays and Lesbians in the Book Trade. Self-satirical this could hardly have been. Was it, however imprudent,

*He has since shown me a photograph of the cutting.

just too good to pass up? Or ironical, along the lines of 'this is what the outside world will expect us to be, but we are not'? Or quite simply sincere? For glibness, i.e. fluency, is a virtue in a trade embracing writers, publishers, printers, librarians and booksellers. Words can often be best understood by reference to their opposites; and dictionaries of synonyms and antonyms, which give 'easy, ready, voluble' among synonyms for 'glib', list among its antonyms 'hesitant, indecisive, vacillating, mute, tongue-tied, incommunicative'. No one marked by even one of those traits would last long in the book trade. So, after all, no irony.

Or no more than resides in the CIA's motto, inscribed on its headquarters in Langley, Virginia: 'And ye shall know the truth, and the truth shall make you free.' The original speaker of those words was not believed by his listeners, who reckoned they were free already—and, since he was about to be stoned, he betook himself off.

*

'How weak a thing is poetry?' said Donne, 'and yet poetry is a counterfeit creation, and makes things that are not, as though they were.' Irony can make things that are, if not as though they were not, then as though they were something quite different. It operates in the (ostensible) overturning of common assumptions in Marvell's 'To his Coy Mistress', when a solemn and resounding passage to do with Time's winged chariot, deserts of eternity, beauty, virginity, worms, dust and ashes, modulates into the reflection that while the grave, as we all know, is a fine and private place, what point is there in fineness and privacy if it can't be used for amorous assignations?

In a similar spirit is the poet's explanation, in 'The Garden', of why Adam was given Eve as a companion. To live alone in Eden, enjoying a double paradise, was just too good for a mere mortal; his inordinate raptures had to be moderated by the attachment of a mate.

42

> After a place so pure, and sweet,
> What other help could yet be meet!

The implication is that Eve was as much a hindrance as a helpmate; and eventually an embarrassment to the point—so the story has it—of causing the man's expulsion from his blissful home. Eden proved too good for Adam, whether alone or accompanied. Earlier in the poem the claim was made, casually but confidently, that the older god Apollo chased Daphne, not for the vulgar purpose of popular belief, but to ensure that she would improve herself into a laurel. Women are made by you and me, but only a god can make a tree.

Though overtly so unlike, a gnashing of teeth in place of a happy celebration of 'fair quiet', Donne's 'Twickenham Garden' is a companion piece to Marvell's poem. To make his garden a thoroughly authentic Paradise, Donne has brought the serpent along with him. (Marvell's lines, 'Stumbling on melons, as I pass, / Insnar'd with flow'rs, I fall on grass', give Empson to observe that 'melon' is Greek for apple, and to link the word darkly with 'fall' and with 'grass' as in 'all flesh is grass'. The reading is ingenious, but knocks the poem sadly askew. We have already seen English apples, in a proleptically Newtonian appearance, falling ripely about the poet's head. It could, I suppose, be argued that Marvell is here reclaiming Milton's lost Garden for man by the deliberate and ironic use of such references, but isn't there enough in the poem already?) Like Marvell's, Donne's trees must be beautiful, for he would want to stay, except that they would mock him. His trouble is unrequited love, honestly and unequivocally unrequited it would seem. And the poem's close is unequivocally ironic:

> O perverse sex, where none is true but she,
> Who's therefore true, because her truth kills me.

The 'sex' is 'perverse' because it offers him plenty of what he doesn't want and withholds precisely what he desires. The only faithful woman he can find is faithful to another. And he is sure of her faithfulness: it has been proved upon his pulse, it is costing him his life.

I wonder whether it was of one of these poems that an Australian student, invited to discuss the workings of irony in seventeenth-century verse, asserted that 'the poem *knows* it's a bad poem, and that is the point of the irony'.

*

'The true end of satire is the amendment of vices by correction': Dryden's manner is too magisterial for irony. If we get an impression of irony in the splendid, living portraits of Shaftesbury and Buckingham, it comes from the blend of what Johnson called 'acrimony of censure' and what looks like commendation or at least a degree of sympathy. Achitophel is 'false', 'for close designs and crooked counsels fit', yet even so, 'sagacious, bold, and turbulent of wit'; diagnosis of his case leads to the conclusion that great wits must surely be near allied to madness. And Zimri is

> A man so various, that he seem'd to be
> Not one, but all mankind's epitome

—good or bad? Hardly good, since he is 'stiff in opinions, always in the wrong', but another interesting case all the same . . .

All of this, we tell ourselves, cannot be true, therefore some of it must be ironic, in the simple sense of intending the contrary of what is said. But we shall reason thus only if we expect satirists to be consistent, all of a piece, in their condemnation, and careful to avoid any suspicion of shilly-shallying, however energetic.

The tip is given in the prefatory note to the reader. The tone is indeed magisterial, but in the fashion of the physician rather than the judge. The satirist, Dryden writes, is no more an enemy to the offender than is the physician to the patient. Sometimes you have to be cruel to be kind. In these particular cases the physician is obliged to prescribe 'harsh remedies'. Achitophel's fiery soul is having a deleterious effect on his frail body, while the manic-depressive Zimri is in rather worse condition. We may feel that neither is likely to be 'corrected' into health, but that is another matter. If Dryden succeeds as a poet he will be prepared to fail as a physician.

44

Perhaps the nearest approach to irony, in spots, comes in the more relaxed passages of *The Medal*, where it is said of the Whig enemies of Charles II that according to their principles God himself would not be safe:

> his thunder could they shun
> He should be forc'd to crown another Son,

and then of their leader, Shaftesbury, in the same quasi-theological tenor, that his God, if he has any, must be one

> That lets the world and human kind alone;
> A jolly God that passes hours too well
> To promise Heav'n, or threaten us with Hell.

*

When Dryden is writing about long-gone politics we are not all of us sure what to expect. In Clough, irony—or what may be admitted as such—takes the form of a thwarting of fairly commonplace expectations. One of the sections in *Amours de Voyage* (1849) opens with a conventional and solemn fanfare, in which even that devious locution 'no doubt' seems not to be sounding its faintly discordant note:

> *Dulce* it is, and *decorum*, no doubt, for the country to fall,—to
> Offer one's blood an oblation to Freedom, and die for the Cause,

and then, while preserving the stately movement, takes a strange turn:

> Still, individual culture is also something, and no man
> Finds quite distinct the assurance that he of all others is called on,
> Or would be justified, even, in taking away from the world that
> Precious creature, himself . . .

No doubt individual culture is *something* (the best people have told us so), and we tend to turn hard of hearing when 'called on' to do far lesser things than offer our blood—but isn't 'precious' going it a bit?

'The Latest Decalogue' is totally ironic, in similar fashion, in

giving bad reasons (though, as we say, good reason) for obeying
the commandments, or at least for not breaking them:

> Thou shalt have one God only; who
> Would be at the expense of two?

and

> Do not adultery commit;
> Advantage rarely comes of it.

The poem is beautifully neat, and telling, but not tricky; after the
second line the reader cannot be in any doubt as to its intention.

The mephistophelean Spirit of *Dipsychus*, behaving like a
romantic poet or a tourist brochure, urges a visit to the Lido,

> That none may say we didn't see
> The ground which Byron used to ride on,

adding, much in Byron's manner,

> And do I don't know what beside on.

Could this piece of sublime-and-ridiculous possibly qualify as
romantic irony? The speaker would be tickled to think that what
he intended as mildly discomfiting smut might be taken for something grander. During his statutory essay in the way of sexual
temptation the Spirit has already described to the dithering
Dipsychus how a Venetian girl's chamber, 'où vous faites votre
affaire', stands 'nicely fitted up for prayer':

> The calm Madonna o'er your head
> Smiles, *col bambino*, on the bed
> Where—but your chaste ears I must spare—
> Where, as we said, *vous faites votre affaire.*

'Christ is risen!' In a scene which imitates or perhaps parodies
Goethe, with the happy non-thinkers all out in the streets
celebrating Easter Sunday, or celebrating on Easter Sunday,
Dipsychus—doing his best to be Faust—proclaims mournfully,

> Ashes to Ashes, Dust to Dust;
> As of the Unjust also of the Just—
> Yea, of that Just One too!

This leads his Mephistopheles to muse,

> H'm! and the tone then after all
> Something of the ironical?
> Sarcastic, say; or were it fitter
> To style it the religious bitter?

—thus adverting to some of the problems facing the taxonomist.

In the amusing Epilogue the poet's uncle confesses that he hasn't very well understood what the poem is all about and he may have dropped into a doze while the 'young man' was soliloquizing, but—he himself is a gently ironical old codger—he allows that much of what 'the devil' has said would have been sensible enough 'if only it hadn't been for the way he said it, and that it was he who said it'.

The uncle might have been in sympathy, if only it hadn't been for this and that, with a lot of what Clough said in his sad and funny fashion. We close with a sad and heartfelt reflection on things as they are, from that super-Prufrockian poem, the *Amours*:

> If there is any one thing in the world to preclude all kindness,
> It is the need of it,—it is this sad, self-defeating dependence.

Or Only Funny and Sad?

WHEN the narrator of Philip Larkin's 'I Remember, I Remember' speaks of the bracken

> where I never trembling sat,
> Determined to go through with it; where she
> Lay back, and 'all became a burning mist',

he is plainly being ironic about the 'burning mist', a famous literary phenomenon of the more reticent past. We know by this stage that he is sending up the Biography, or come to that the Autobiography, of the Poet, a form of art in which everything that happens is frightfully significant. (Or gets dragged regardless into the pretentious area.) But he is also talking about his actual unspent youth; he never suffered the cliché, but neither did he enjoy the experience. Funny in its expertly selected incidentals, the poem in its totality is a sad one; nothing like so frivolous as a mere dig at prosaic old Coventry, for what didn't happen there could have failed to happen anywhere.

A particularly knotty problem—what happened happened in a very precise place—is posed by Peter Reading's poem, 'Cub', which first appeared in *The Times Literary Supplement* of 23 March 1984. The poem is spoken, so to speak, by a Reuters reporter in Sidon who sees 'a slight soldier/homunculus' firing at 'a fat juicy jeep of Israelis'. One of the Israeli soldiers is hit, and their assailant is then gunned down. 'Well,' the poem ends,

> nobody looks for a *motive* from these Old Testament shitters—
> thick hate is still in the genes. I learned the boy was aged 12.

48

There followed letters of angry protest, among them one from Israel and one signed by six academics of assorted nationalities and races, condemning the poem as 'a straightforwardly anti-Semitic statement'. *The Times Literary Supplement* defended the publication, opining that the title of the poem was applicable not only to the twelve-year-old boy but also to the reporter: i.e. one couldn't expect much from him in the way of subtlety. (He claims to have spent six months already in 'parched mad bloody Lebanon'; and I would rather have supposed the reference was to some putative old saying about the wisdom of killing the cub before it was fully grown.)

Other letters defended the poem, for example as a 'persona' piece for whose views the author accepted no responsibility. And the publisher of Peter Reading's collections, himself a 'deeply committed Jew', brought up the old joke that, like the red flag carried in front of the first motor cars, perhaps some distinctive signal ought to precede a passage of irony. He saw 'Cub' as satirizing the recently expressed view that Israel's invasion of Lebanon equalled the Holocaust. (It could well have been this view that exacerbated the reactions of the objectors.) Adducing the reference to the italicized '*motive*', another correspondent interpreted the poem as an indictment—always safe, this—of the mass media and of our passive response to those media.

Less disastrous than a letter-bomb, though not a subtle form of literary criticism or political debate, were the gifts of excreta received at the offices of the periodical. Seemingly no representations came in from Palestinian sources. And, wisely, Peter Reading kept his silence.

I have to admit that the objections seemed to me stronger, certainly less far-fetched, than the attempts to refute them. The poem doesn't strike me as ironic. (Not that one would presume to exempt Jews, who might be thought to have invented irony, from its attentions.) Nor do I think it anti-Semitic, straightforwardly or insinuatingly. Possibly something has gone amiss with the poem, its harshness stepped up to avoid the easy horrors-of-war routine: 'Old Testament shitters' can embrace both factions, though the reporter must be more juvenile than a 'cub' if he is ignorant of the motives of either faction. There are always motives, however insufficient or perversely self-damaging they appear to later or uninvolved observers. And—since one isn't going to take it as a compelling sign of greater civilization that in Israel the age of conscription is later—the closing reference to the boy's youth works like a thumb stuck in the pan of the scales.

I found the poem bitter and disgusted and sad—angry with all concerned (they kill) and, less distinctly, sorry for them all (they get killed). Tone is a fearfully difficult thing not to get wrong, short of doing without it altogether. Who can be wise, amazed, temperate and furious, loyal and neutral, in a moment—and tactful as well? But I am not a Jew.

Ironies Which Aren't

IT is probably a mistake to see irony in the Grampus's remark that 'I sometimes forget I *am* absent-minded, and remember everything.' Yet the sentence would qualify if addressed to someone who had confidently relied on the speaker to forget that he was owed money—and the more clearly if accompanied by an ironical smile. (This latter, Muecke surmises, is 'perhaps more frequent in novels than in life'.) It's a question of context. And likewise with Erik Satie's crack, 'un touriste est quelqu'un qui habite une tour', which would assume more meaning if we could suppose him to have had in mind those towering modern hotels in the gorgeous East where the tourist can experience all the peculiar 'culture' of the country without venturing out of the premises. As it is, we must read it as a specimen of surrealism rather than a piece of realism.

And concerning De Quincey's habit of spending the time in which he could have finished an overdue article on writing long and beautiful letters to *Blackwood's Magazine* to explain why he couldn't finish it on time, as noted by Alethea Hayter—any odour of irony vanishes at the recognition that there are times when all one can manage to write is letters, a minor form of unwanted literary art; they relieve one temporarily of (to borrow a phrase from De Quincey) 'the burden of the incommunicable'. De Quincey's pleasantry about indulgence in murder leading ineluctably, step by step, to robbery, drinking, sabbath-breaking, and procrastination, still has some point; which cannot be said for the ancient joke concerning the farmer who, discovering his young son in the hay-loft with a milkmaid, cuffed him about the head and shouted, 'Next you'll be smoking!' The relative shift on the scale of sinfulness between cigarettes and sex has made this incomprehensible to a new generation.

'Every reader will have the greatest difficulty detecting irony that mocks his own beliefs or characteristics.' So writes Wayne C. Booth. Also, one might add, in detecting simple sincerity in those circumstances. Booth tells of a student of his who wrote a paper describing the joys of deer-hunting and the thrill he felt as he cut the deer's throat and watched the life dying in its 'large, beautiful, child-like eyes'. Professor Booth took for granted that the student was satirizing blood sports, but in conference with him discovered that he was being entirely sincere, not to say enthusiastic.*

*At the London hotel where Dan Jacobson stayed on arriving from South Africa, there was 'a caricature of the hanging, flogging Englishman', Jacobson's first encounter with a live exemplar of 'the English flair for self-imitation', the zeal with which the English conform to types so familiar in literature that 'the outsider positively expects some "real" man buried within the type to give him a secret wink of irony, a little gesture or nod of complicity'. He adds that the other residents indicated neither agreement nor disagreement with the

A sort of enthusiasm is visible in an incident Stephen Spender recounts in his *Journals 1939–1983* (1985), concerning an interview he gave to a student magazine at the University of Cincinnati in 1953. Having seen the typescript, he objected to a supposed confession as to why in his youth he had joined the Communist Party—namely, to get published. The editor explained breezily that what the magazine wanted was plain facts. When Spender pointed out that the so-called facts were wrong, the editor declared that this didn't matter, they just wanted *facts*, right or wrong. The chairman of the English Department then argued that students would have read all about Spender's political past already, but the editor easily put him down: 'Our readers never read.'

Yes, the academic life . . . During the 1960s (and, I dare say, at other times and elsewhere) staff promotions in the University of Singapore depended solely on publications, or in some cases on services to the country. The English Department, as remote from professional magazines as from serving the State, was exceptionally disadvantaged in the matter. Some of us proposed that staff members' talents and achievements as teachers should also be taken into account. Whereupon the then Vice-Chancellor put an end to the discussion by saying: 'But *all* university teachers are good teachers.' What dissuaded me from believing this was said ironically was only the fact that the Vice-Chancellor, a Chinese economist, had to my knowledge never before indulged in public irony.

Some twenty years ago a survey of the *œuvre* of Mary Stewart appeared in the *New Statesman*. This, I was told recently, was actually a satirical send-up of the author and her popular romantic thrillers, but many readers had taken it as straight-faced praise. On looking into the article, I found it in fairly plain fact a lively and measured appreciation, evincing merely the odd minor

---

man's views, loudly expressed over the breakfast table, but managed to convey by their silence that it wasn't the views they disapproved of so much as the vehemence with which he voiced them.

and mild possible irony: chiefly when the critic, F. W. J. Hemmings, drew a parallel between Mrs Stewart's expertise in the kitchen and her skill in the confection of her novels. Mrs Stewart had been pleased by the article, and understandably so.

Instead of a case of irony taken or mis-taken *au pied de la lettre* by the dim-witted, this turned out to be something more pleasing —a case of a serious, honest statement misread as irony by the sophisticated. The critic informs me that he genuinely enjoyed reading the novels 'all at one gulp' and was unaware of being satirical. And since the tone of the article doesn't in the least invite an ironical interpretation, the theory of the intentional fallacy (or, 'never trust the artist, trust the tale') has no bearing here. Those sophisticated persons were led astray by their rooted preconceptions. No serious-sounding critique of a romantic novelist could conceivably be meant seriously; certainly not when it was printed in a serious-minded paper; even more surely not when its writer was a university professor, member of a class serious-minded by definition. (But see p. 55 upcoming.) The only irony here lies in cleverness deceiving itself.

*

There is a type of irony which one recognizes only with the help of hindsight, because only later does the irony come into being. As when Byron wrote to Lady Melbourne, a month after marrying Annabella Milbanke and a year before their separation, that 'we may win the Dunmow flitch of bacon for anything I know'. Some four years later he assured his half-sister Augusta Leigh, of the affair with the Countess Guiccioli, that it was troublesome but 'there are hopes that we may quarrel'; the relationship lasted until his death. Admittedly that occurred only five years later. And admittedly he may have felt it fit to soft-pedal in his report to Augusta.

In Book 3 of *Gargantua and Pantagruel* the praises are sung at length of a wonder herb, Pantagruelion, which begins as hemp and then, since it is miraculously unconsumed by fire, is given the name 'asbestos'. 'O chose grande! chose admirable!' 'What a great and wonderful thing it is!' Only in recent years has this 'blessed' product been unmasked as a killer. Had Rabelais's contemporary readers known its true nature, this would have been an instance of the famous 'dramatic' or 'tragic' irony.

Lest this should sound mean and negative, let us observe that here as elsewhere ironies can work the other way about. Fire was either a gift—ambiguous, 'as what gods give must be'—or else stumbled on by accident. (See Lamb on the origins of roast pork.) The stone that the builders refused becomes the corner-stone; and the discovery of penicillin began from a blob of mould noticed on a discarded culture plate. However, the jacket of a 1984 biography of Sir Alexander Fleming, with an aptness not always achieved in blurbs, informs us that neither as a scientist nor as a man was he 'cast in a heroic mould'.

*

In David Lodge's *Small World* (1984) a character called Philip Swallow tells fellow academic Morris Zapp how once, when he was abroad lecturing for the British Council, his plane was forced to return to Genoa because of a fire in one of the engines. He spent the night there, in the bed of a British Council wife whose husband was absent, no doubt on cultural business. She and her husband and their son, he adds, were killed in an air crash the following year. A sad story, Zapp comments. 'Ironic, too, isn't it, when you think of how we met?' says Swallow.

Why ironic? Tragic in the second part of the story, and a mildly odd coincidence, since there were planes in both parts. But scarcely ironic. (No wonder that an Italian academic in the novel exclaims, 'Ooh, the English and their ironies! You never know where you are with them.') It might, implausibly, be deemed ironic that Swallow later discovers that the woman wasn't actually killed, and resumes the affair with her. Or is this merely a coincidence accidentally discredited?

The more forceful irony, some people may reckon, is that the academics in the novel spend so much time and energy on travelling to conferences (seeing, as Douglas Johnson put it recently in reviewing a French publication called *Homo academicus*, more air hostesses than students), writing their esoteric articles and books, and sleeping around, that they can have little of either commodity left over for what some people have supposed their primary function: teaching the young. The author has—not, I imagine, deliberately—secured his rear against attack by this irony with a nice one of his own, maybe inspired by Wilde. Zapp states that he has given up screwing around: 'I came to the conclusion that sex is a sublimation of the work instinct.'

To suggest for a moment that any irony resided in the fact that the author of this devastating exposé (?) of Eng. lit. academics is himself an Eng. lit. academic would be to betray oneself as a spoilsport, prude and hypocrite . . . And as a simpleton, for who takes novels seriously? In any case, *Small World* is a very clever book, and academics are meant to be clever.

'We are significance-seeking organisms,' as Michael Frayn has it. The trouble with accidents is that they are accidental, they lack import, they won't suffice. So we have developed conventions, in literature and in life, 'which permit us to extract emotional flavouring from the most irrelevant of contingencies'.* The narrator of Julian Barnes's *Flaubert's Parrot*, by coincidence published in the same year as *Small World*, opines that 'one way of legitimizing coincidences, of course, is to call them ironies'. He continues: 'Irony is, after all, the modern mode, a drinking companion for resonance and wit. Who could be against it? And yet sometimes I wonder if the wittiest, most resonant irony isn't just a well-brushed, well-educated coincidence.'

---

*Space-time correlates, however trumped up, 'do seem to bear some charge of meaning,' Frayn continues, giving this illustration: 'The street where the man was shot—I passed it not two weeks previously! And the place the shot was fired from was *almost exactly* where forty years ago the man's grandfather used to run a jellied eel stall!'

What the Bible Tells Us

IRONY—which, we have seen, doesn't cast out seriousness—must surely lurk in the parable, Luke 16, of the unjust, or cunning, or—God helps him who helps himself—admirably shrewd steward. Finding the parable so difficult of exposition, and more likely to do harm than good, J. F. Powers's Father Urban wondered whether Jesus might not have been a little tired when he delivered it.

We seem to be on firmer ground when, in the Gospel according to St Matthew, Jesus tells a young man that if he wishes to be perfect, he should 'go and sell that thou hast, and give to the poor, and thou shalt have treasure in heaven'. Since the young man is well off, the advice upsets him, thus eliciting the famous saying about the camel and the eye of a needle.

In St John, it is Judas Iscariot who asks why the ointment with which Mary of Bethany anoints Jesus's feet shouldn't be sold and the proceeds, which he estimates as three hundred pence, donated to the poor. To which Jesus replies: 'Let her alone . . . For the poor always ye have with you; but me ye have not always.' It can be assumed that Christ was perfect to begin with, and already had treasure in heaven, and so needed to make no sacrifice at the moment. Either way his answer is unforgettable; this is one of those sudden and brilliant occasions, paradoxical epiphanies, when he shows himself a true Son of Man, standing out from the unco guid characters, both the genuine and the false, who surround him. If he is at fault here, it is, like that larger one, a happy fault. The Son of God ought once in a while to have his feet anointed, especially in view of what is to happen to them later. (He would have been aware of that irony voiced by the future first

Christian martyr, Stephen, in Anthony Burgess's *The Kingdom of the Wicked*, 1985: 'We believe in the coming of the Messiah, but anyone who claims to be the Messiah is condemned and put to death.'*) Jesus's saying, we note, is politically reactionary: unlike him, the poor will always be around, poverty isn't going to be abolished.

Further irony is present in the version of St Luke, where the ointment is dispensed by an unnamed woman, 'a sinner', i.e. a prostitute (how else could a woman sin?). The Pharisee reasons that Jesus cannot be a prophet since a prophet would know what sort of woman this was and send her packing. Jesus replies with a short parable: those who are forgiven most will love their forgiver most.

In his next words the order of events is turned about: 'Her sins, which are many, are forgiven; for she loved much.' Both propositions are perfectly valid, the firsst worldly-wise, the second heavenly. Also, Jesus points out mischievously, his host certainly hasn't kissed his feet or anointed them, or even given him water to wash them in.

'The poor always ye have with you.' A similarly pessimistic pronouncement is made by Parnell, in Yeats's poem of that name, when he tells 'a cheering man' that 'Ireland shall get her freedom / And you still break stone.' Such ironies have their point at a time when in some parts of the world it is believed that human dignity forbids men to break stone. It is true that machines will do it for us, just as in another age our servants (or the servants of some select souls) would do our living for us. But what will men do instead? Inactivity is a very considerable indignity, and it would be ironic if, instead of perishing as a result of splitting the atom, mankind died out because of its principled disinclination to break stone.

*

*Kierkegaard wrote in his Journals that for a Christian irony is not enough because it can never answer to the terrible truth that salvation entails the crucifixion of God. True, irony is never enough, for anyone. Yet, one is inclined to interpose, many others have been crucified, without the benefit of being God.

'. . . every idle word that men shall speak, they shall give account thereof in the day of judgement.' Very early on was the Word, and the Testaments have a lot to say about words. But it is all too easy to wax satirical over what latter-day translators have made of the Bible and the Prayer Book. Possibly God is partly to blame, as Nietzsche suggests in *Beyond Good and Evil*: 'It is a curious thing that God learned Greek when he wished to turn author—and that he did not learn it better.' And after all, Richard Whately, Archbishop of Dublin in the first half of the nineteenth century, was correct in advising his underlings: 'Never forget, gentlemen, that this is not the Bible. This, gentlemen, is only a translation of the Bible.'

In the Revised Standard Version (1946), Mary of Bethany no longer warns bystanders that, since Lazarus has been dead for four days, he is likely to 'stink'; she murmurs demurely that 'there will be an odour'. In the Jerusalem Bible (1966), instead of it ceasing to be with Sarah 'after the manner of women', we hear that her monthly periods have ceased.*

The first of these changes is a euphemism (the word 'stink' smells bad), intended to render the reference more acceptable—to whom? The second accords with the prime aim (we take it) of the revisers: to make the sacred writings more readily comprehensible to modern readers or listeners. The phrase 'after the manner of women' could signify no end of eccentricities or worse! What might be thought hard to understand is the revisers' simple faith in the virtues of understanding: that is, I hasten to add, in this mysterious sphere. But perhaps, with so many intransigent mysteries bedevilling Christianity, they thought, let's at least call menstruation 'periods'.

The hymn which begins 'There is a green hill far away, / Without a city wall' caught my imagination at an early age. Other green hills all had city walls, only this one was without. Poor deprived green hill! No wonder it was 'Where the dear Lord was crucified / Who died to save us all'. One's obscure pity for the

*See Peter Mullen, 'The Religious Speak-Easy', in *Fair of Speech: The Uses of Euphemism*, 1985.

green hill (or, as I took it then, greenhill, something more special than the green hills common in Warwickshire) carried over into sorrow for the dear Lord, who had also been unfairly treated.

I misunderstood, there as elsewhere, but I was captured; and to be captured is more important than to understand. Understanding can come later.

*

Theology is fairly remote from the Bible, and more so from Christ. In this present aspect it would require a book to itself, though not necessarily deserve one.

God moves in a mysterious way, not only (which is fair enough) to perform his wonders, but as affects the performing of horrors. By definition, evil cannot come from God, therefore it must come from somewhere or someone else. Not all evil can be attributed to man, to man's abuse of his free will; and even if it could . . .? Yet the assigning of too much power to the Devil cannot be reconciled with God's omnipotence, while the assigning of too little cannot be reconciled with God's love and mercy. The problem has kept theologians in work for centuries—among their high-minded squirmings being the notion that the Devil's freedom to do evil couldn't be abridged without abridging his freedom to do good—practically, indeed, until they gave up religious studies in favour of social work. The availability as fall-back of this latter occupation takes the sting out of the fear professed by Swift in *Argument against Abolishing Christianity* that the repealing of the religion might just conceivably put the Church at risk. More to the point, George Moore's facetious witticism, 'The Church is divine, She even survives the clergy', is no longer facetious, and promises to be untrue.

'The ways of God are strange!' exclaimed the unironic Bishop in Siegfried Sassoon's poem, ' "They" '. How strange is illustrated by an Islamic story that Jeffrey Burton Russell recounts in his book, *Lucifer: The Devil in the Middle Ages* (1984). A child and a grown-up are in Heaven, where, though both died in the True Faith, the grown-up occupies a higher place. God explains that this is because the man has done many good works, whereupon the child asks why God allowed him to die before he too could do good. God answers that he knew the child would grow up to be a sinner, and therefore it was better that he should die young. At this, a massed cry arises from the depths of Hell: 'Why, O Lord!, did You not let *us* die before we became sinners?'

The assertion that God's judgements are unsearchable, as St Paul has it, and his ways past finding out sounds like a handy cop-out, and has often been employed as an all-purpose bromide, an auxiliary of 'pie in the sky'. To hear it mouthed must have created many a young atheist. ('Still an atheist . . . thank God,' said Luis Buñuel.) In the course of *The Dynasts*, the Spirit of the Years explains to his colleagues, as they contemplate the crowning of Napoleon in Milan Cathedral, that the rites are connected with 'a local cult, called Christianity'; to which the Spirit of the Pities replies that he hadn't recognized it, though in its 'early, lovingkindly days' it had meant much to him.

In Anatole France's *The Revolt of the Angels*, when an old lady asks how he would explain the existence of plagues, famines and earthquakes, a priest answers, with a heavenly smile: 'It is surely necessary that God should sometimes remind us of his existence.' (Which we might have supposed was the priest's job.) Perhaps with Voltaire's epigram in mind, Stendhal—as reported by Mérimée—went further: 'What excuses God is that he does not exist.'

It remains true, though, that if there is a God, both his ends and his means may well be mysteries to us, who cannot see the final outcome. The hymn of Cowper's which begins 'God moves in a mysterious way' continues by warning us not to judge the Lord by feeble sense: 'God is his own interpreter, / And he will make it plain.' We would not wish to figure as pathetically as Lieutenant Scheisskopf's wife, in Joseph Heller's *Catch-22* (1961), when she is exposed to Yossarian's view of God as not so much working in mysterious ways as not working at all. He asks her why she is getting upset since she doesn't believe in God anyway. 'I don't,' she sobs. 'But the God I don't believe in is a good God, a just God, a merciful God. He's not the mean and stupid God you make him out to be.'

Nor would we want to be mistaken for A. A. Cleary's emblematic poet, compassionate but irreligious, who, having looked around him, decides that 'his own compassion is superior to any he can imagine, *to any ultimate one*: if *he* were God, he would not allow such suffering, so there is no God. Then he makes much of his own compassion.'* No such solipsistic solecism was committed by the Israeli Interior Minister, a rabbi, who explained that twenty-two children were killed in a road accident because the Sabbath was desecrated in Israel: 'This tragedy was not caused by chance. It was the hand of God.' (Reuters report, *The Times*, 24 June 1985.) There speaks the true voice of the omniscient fundamentalist. 'Kill the lot—God will recognize his own,' the papal legate is alleged to have pronounced regarding the wholesale massacre of the inhabitants of Béziers during the crusade against the Albigensians.

However, it seems worth noting that St Paul echoed the word used (in English and in Greek) by one of Job's comforters: God 'doeth great things and unsearchable'. The same, Eliphaz the Temanite, asked Job if he supposed it was 'any pleasure to the Almighty that thou art righteous?' But it was also he who finally incurred the brunt of the Lord's wrath, in that 'ye have not spoken of me the thing that is right'. Perhaps the Lord wasn't altogether happy to have been searched out as unsearchable.

Emerson cautioned us against speaking too much of God, for thought will desert us. And possibly both Mrs Cleary and the Poet are wasting their time in wrangling over old, forgotten wars. Booth cites an obscure irony concocted by Samuel Butler some hundred years ago, in *Erewhon*: 'Once I had to leap down a not inconsiderable waterfall into a deep pool below, and my swag was so heavy that I was very nearly drowned. I had indeed a hairbreadth escape; but, as luck would have it, Providence was on my side.' Only those aware of an ancient distinction between

---

*The poor fellow is in the position identified by Elias Canetti: 'The man who doesn't believe in God takes all the guilt of the world upon himself.'

capital-P Providence and luck will perceive the joke, the satirical dig at the Church. For most younger readers today, I imagine, the statement must appear merely tautologous, a defect of style, as if to say 'luckily I was lucky'. Butler might be thought to have been hoist with his own petard. It is a risk that all verbal engineers run.

*

'The most scandalous charges were suppressed,' Gibbon observed in connection with the trial of Pope John XXIII, Baldassare Cossa, whom we might have expected to be a right holy man, and 'the vicar of Christ was only accused of piracy, murder, rape, sodomy, and incest'. 'Only' can very nearly be a one-word irony.

Quite different is the trial and testing of Raju, the uncertain hero of R. K. Narayan's novel, *The Guide* (1958). It is his fate, in William Walsh's summary, to be 'the product of other people's convictions', 'a projection of what people need'. He is 'an Indian specification of that human type in whom character exists with a certain formlessness. Its deliquescence is arrested only by a lead from outside.' He has lived by his wits, helped by the protean qualities of his nature. When sent to prison for some minor offence, he finds himself perfectly happy.

> Now I realized that people generally thought of me as being unsound and worthless, not because I deserved the label but because they had been seeing me in the wrong place all along. To appreciate me they should have come to the Central Jail and watched me.

He has gained a function and achieved a status there, as teacher, comforter, gardener, and secretary.

Soon after his unwanted release ('If this was prison life, why didn't more people take to it?') he is spotted loitering in a neglected temple by a peasant, in need of a holy man, who promptly takes him for a holy man. (A simple irony, but ironies more complex and profound are to follow.) There, evidently, is his new livelihood. When he forgets how to end a sacred story or complete a moral, it doesn't bother his disciples: it is his presence they require, not his logic. He grows influential and useful among the villagers, but still feels guilty about the imposture.

A drought has set in, and through a conjunction of accident and misunderstanding compounded by his fear of exposure, Raju is trapped or traps himself into undertaking a fast to bring rain. The newspapers and the government take him up and he attains to the vulgar fame that attaches itself to film stars. Yet the expectations and needs (and illusions) of others are creating a true swami out of him. 'If by avoiding food I should help the trees bloom, and the grass grow, why not do it thoroughly?' And he enters into a fast unto death from which even the government doctors cannot dissuade him.

*

A final solution to the problems of sin, poverty, freedom, unemployment and leisure is proposed by Diderot, taking his tip from Swift, in *Conversation with the Abbé Barthélemy*. In order to save them from the half-certainty—at a conservative estimate—of eternal torment, babies should be dispatched as soon as possible after baptism.

The Fortunes of Faust

NOTHING, we think, could be more pertinent than the story of Faust, the dissatisfied or visionary academic who sold his immortal soul to the Devil in return for . . . But we have to start again—the sundry stories of Faust, since in his appearances through the ages he has bartered the joys of heaven (or sacrificed his comfort and reputation) for, variously, the power to do good to others,

Prometheanly or in the manner of the Countess Cathleen; for the power that corrupts; for the knowledge that it is man's right or even duty to acquire; for the knowledge of what it is not given to man, even a professor, to know; for money and sex; for a full and exuberant life in the style of Renaissance man; for a life of worldly vanity and unsanctified glamour . . . And was consequently damned and dragged down howling into hell; or was not.

Given the Devil's well-attested trickiness, his penchant for turning noble aspirations into petty fiascos and fine longings into mean lusts, the potentialities for irony are vast. Yet, except in Thomas Mann's hands, and unlike the opportunities for folksy slapstick and small-time magic, they have not been turned to very much account. First the Church frowned on such dealings, and then the Enlightenment discountenanced them.

*

The initial ambitions of Marlowe's Faustus are a curiously mixed lot. 'A sound magician is a mighty god', and with the help of magic he will 'resolve me of all ambiguities' (thus putting paid to many future thinkers and all ironists), study strange philosophies (the ordinary sort is 'odious and obscure'), wall all Germany with brass, dress the students bravely in silk, have himself crowned king, and invent strange engines of war. What in the event he gets is a devil dressed like a woman and begirt with exploding fireworks, a homely pageant representing the Seven Deadly Sins (he won't have time actually to commit them), a stale lecture on astronomy, a recital by blind Homer, the privilege of boxing the Pope's ear and of cheating a horse-coper, and the thrill of gratifying a pregnant duchess with out-of-season grapes.

Brilliant bursts of irony there are: in Faust's misjudgement of Mephistophilis on first meeting him ('How pliant . . . Full of obedience and humility!'); when he exhorts Mephistophilis to stop lamenting the loss of everlasting bliss and learn 'manly fortitude' from him; in his exclamation, 'O, might I see hell, and return again, / How happy were I then!'; when he asks Helen to make him immortal with a kiss (cf. his later recognition, 'O, no

64

end is limited to damned souls!') and cries, 'Her lips suck forth my soul: see, where it flies!' But, no matter how heretical or progressive Marlowe may have been in his private ideas, the great and moving passages, whether spoken by Faust or by Mephistophilis, have to do with hell and damnation.

As for those aspirations of Faustus's, two of them have been realized by succeeding magicians. Part of Germany has been walled, though not necessarily with brass, and very strange engines of war have been invented.

*

What promises to be a fully-fledged example of the commonest ironic deployment—the deflating of self-importance—occurs in the Prologue (in Heaven) to Goethe's *Faust*. Mephistopheles considers himself no end of a devil, the great and gleeful naysayer, busily twisting good intentions into deplorable outcomes. The Lord, however, gives a very different account of him, and (as nobleness obliges) to his face: Mephistopheles is a useful sidekick who stings slothful man into activity and, though (or perhaps because) he is the Devil, must perforce create. Confirmation of this might be seen in a 'fragment' in the periodical *Das Athenäum* (1798), where Friedrich Schlegel points out that Satan was a great favourite with German poets and philosophers and so must have his good side; despite his fondness for destroying, confusing, and leading astray, he was frequently to be found in the best society.

The wager follows: Mephistopheles is at liberty to tempt Faust as sorely as he wishes, yet—the Lord maintains—no matter how this representative man gropes and stumbles, he will still follow the true path. (Later this term appears to have been tacitly modified to read: not go all the way down the path of evil.)

Consequently it will be taken as a sign of Mephistopheles' invincible complacency that, when the Lord and his retinue have withdrawn, he should joke about how he enjoys calling on the Old Man now and then and how handsome it is of so important a personage to chat familiarly with the Devil himself. Even so, since in conversation Mephistopheles has proved the more entertaining of the two, lively where the Lord is lofty, and more *au fait* with matters in the lower world, more 'one of us', we may reckon—and the more readily these days—that the irony flows in the other direction and it is God who is being put in his place.

Mephistopheles' prepotency, as we may see it, is reinforced on his first appearance to Faust, when he defines himself with some dignity as a part of the power which always wills evil and always procures good. At first hearing he seems to be repeating and assenting to the Lord's lowering description of him and his function. But his following speeches give the declaration a different slant. He explains that he is part (modesty again) of the part that was once the whole: Darkness or Mother Night was the whole, until Light was created out of her, and now threatens to oust her from her original predominance. Mephistopheles wills what *others* regard as evil—the destruction of the Something, the human world (associated with light)—in order to procure what *he* considers good, the restoration of the dark and primal Nothing. The diabolical rebel is an old-fashioned reactionary. Particularly intriguing are those ironies which, unlike tableaux, move and extend themselves and change course.

In the eyes of the student it may constitute a further (and alarmingly gross) irony that Goethe changes course, and the bulk of the huge drama to follow has little to do with either good or evil, but rather more to do with old stories, some vulgar and some grandiose, and much more with its author's changing interests over some sixty years. What could there be in common between the energetic hero who saves Helen, lately of Troy, from Menelaus and has a son by her who resembles Icarus in his behaviour and Lord Byron in his looks, and the petulant and seemingly middle-aged professor of the opening scene? Even though Mephistopheles declares himself at home with the Classical Walpurgis Night, what legitimate link can there be between its sphinxes, griffins, centaurs, and lamiae, and the Job-like homeliness of the Prologue?

Albeit by now we can hardly recall what the war was about, in the end the Lord comes out winner—if only, as most modern readers will think, by a whisker. Or by an act of God, by the arbitrary exercise of divine will (which never looks right in art), seeing that Mephistopheles has just pulled off what ought to have been the decisive feat of turning Faust's good civic intentions, in the shape of land reclamation, into the murder of a harmless old couple while resisting a compulsory purchase order. What—a rightly affronted Mephistopheles might ask as he is pelted with flaming roses and Faust's soul is snatched from under his nose—happened to divine justice?

In one of his final and for the most part undignified utterances Mephistopheles is allowed an allusion—apparently unheard by anyone on stage but affecting us like a brick in the face—to a long-standing but still shocking irony. The most shameful thing the forces of evil could contrive in their campaign to discredit and damn mankind — the Crucifixion—has become the object of devotion for angels as for men. *O felix culpa* . . . On whose head this irony falls is not certain. Which means we cannot dismiss the matter, it lingers questioningly in our minds.

By a quasi-feminist twist at the very end, in an atmosphere far more that of opera than of miracle play, it is 'the eternal womanly' that (as, we gather, is customary) lifts us on high: namely the Mater Gloriosa, on this particular occasion together with the dolorous infanticide Gretchen. The Lord does not deign to drop in and chat with the assembled company, or even show himself; perhaps in his opinion the fruits of victory have gone astray and he is sulking in his tent; perhaps he has quietly been made redundant. One can appreciate those doubts about Goethe's religious sincerity, for this is not everybody's idea of Christianity. It isn't even everybody's idea of literature.

Shakespearian

WHILE both Faustus and Faust despised the orthodox curricula of their day, the former expected better things from necromantic literature, including the study of strange philosophy, whereas the latter entertained a grudging hope that Mephistopheles would relieve his boredom and frustration by guiding him through the little world and then the great.

Both would have felt some sympathy with Berowne, in *Love's Labour's Lost*, when he objects to Navarre's plan to turn his court into a miniature academe. By restricting themselves to a Spartan diet and three hours sleep a night, and forswearing the company of women, the young gentlemen are to study hard for three years, living in philosophy, as one of them puts it. 'Light seeking light', Berowne contends, 'doth light of light beguile': in plain English, too much reading is bad for the eyes, they grow blind to what is directly in front of them. Better to come forth into the light of things, and let Nature be your teacher, for study, when at last it catches what it was hunting, wins it in the way towns are won by burning them down: 'so won, so lost'.

'How well he's read, to reason against reading!' The King's riposte is aptly directed, but it leaves the objection intact. What wins Berowne over is merely that he has given his word, albeit without having read the small print, or perhaps that he has nothing better to do at the moment. Despite his later speech in praise of women, or their eyes,

> They are the books, the arts, the academes,
> That show, contain, and nourish all the world,

he too stands in need of correction. His puns and mockeries and sophistries are themselves studied, artificial, nothing but words.* And accordingly Rosaline sentences him to spend a remedial twelvemonth among the sick and the dying:

> A jest's prosperity lies in the ear
> Of him that hears it, never in the tongue
> Of him that makes it . . .

Let him see if he can get *them* to laugh.

Rosaline's pronouncement deserves to be studied by the ironist, even though his own ear may quite often be the only one to pay attention to his tongue.

*

While word-play abounds on all levels, there is apparently less irony to be extracted from Shakespeare than one might expect of our national poet. Until—and I don't think it is simply a case of he that seeketh findeth—we look more closely into him.

In *King Lear*, the 'bad' daughter proving good and the 'good' daughters bad is a stock situation, arising from the wilful misapprehension common in fairy-tales, those monuments of realism. It is left to the Fool, innocent insider speaking for sensible outsider, to point wry morals—'Why, this fellow has banish'd two on's daughters, and did the third a blessing against his will'—and he might as well, since he knows he will be whipped anyway, for telling the truth, for lying, or for keeping silent. A fiercer irony, partaking of the appropriate ('poetic justice') instead of the paradoxical, the punishment nicely calculated to fit the crime, is the blinding of Gloucester: the dark and vicious place where he begot Edmund has cost him his eyes.

But wait, the irony turns crude when we examine it—on the lips of Gloucester's legitimate son, Edgar, it is to say the least lacking in delicacy—and then illusory. It was for helping Lear to escape to Dover that Gloucester was blinded, for love of the old King,

---

*For further thoughts on this point see 'A World of Words', *Shakespeare's Wordplay*, M. M. Mahood, 1957.

not because of some ancient lust. Any irony present here is pathetic, not minatory in the Old Testament style. In the course of a book on Shakespeare drawn from classroom experience, I quoted a student's comment, in connection with Gloucester's misjudgement of his two sons, that he was due for an eye-opener before long. And was subsequently reprimanded by one of our leading Shakespeare scholars for being crude.

In another fairy-tale situation, when Leontes is at long last permitted to view the supposed statue of his supposedly dead wife—'a piece many years in doing'—he complains, in so far as he dare complain of anything, that Hermione was not so wrinkled, nothing like as aged as the statue makes out. Paulina explains that the sculptor's art is to have allowed for the sixteen years which have passed since the subject's death and to portray her as she would be if she were alive today. The transformation scene which follows is rich in ironies—Paulina affects to fear they will accuse her of 'unlawful business', of dabbling in witchcraft, but in the present circumstances Leontes is eager to accept magic as 'an art lawful as eating'—and, not in spite of this but all the more because of it, deeply moving.

In *Julius Caesar*, Antony's 'For Brutus is an honourable man; / So are they all, all honourable men' is ironic in its second element; and some time before the sixth repetition of the word 'honourable' in relation to Brutus, it has come to seem totally ironic. Repetition doesn't always strengthen a statement; by providing time for doubt to set in, it can erode or overturn it. Once dead, Brutus is 'the noblest Roman of them all': nothing ironic here, simply the convention of the obituary with some now permissible truth thrown in.

Does this irony reach forward into *Antony and Cleopatra*, where the word 'honour' is fairly frequent on Antony's lips? During his quarrel with Octavius Caesar, he tells Lepidus, 'The honour is sacred which he talks on now, / Supposing that I lacked it'; and Cleopatra had earlier granted, grudgingly, that 'Your honour calls you hence.' The word—these days mostly heard in disputes concerning money—is clearly a dangerous one; it tends to rebound. When the soldiers are discussing the propensity of the great for weeping, Agrippa observes—in a reference to the speech about 'the noblest Roman of them all'—that Antony wept when he found Brutus slain at Philippi, and Enobarbus breaks in to remark that that year Antony was 'troubled with a rheum'. Is there some backward-reaching irony here? But I fear that—as my Singapore students, lovers of moderation, used to say of the conduct of tragic heroes—I am going too far.

In its plot *Macbeth* is essentially ironic. Its hero enumerates and describes with unsurpassable cogency the reasons why, given the means he has chosen and persists in, he cannot possibly succeed in his end—to be a respected, benevolent, and hence beloved ruler. The means and the end are close together, in that this is the shortest and fastest-moving of Shakespeare's tragedies. (The irony is rubbed in by Macbeth's incredulous complaint, immediately after murdering Duncan, that he couldn't say 'amen' though he had 'most need of blessing'.) Macbeth thinks (and to some extent feels) rightly, and acts wrongly. Hence, such irregularities of the human soul being hard to account for in rational terms, comes the temptation to see him as a good but weak man damned in a strong and wicked wife. What happens in Act II, scene II could be held to support this view, or to point to the contrary. Is Lady Macbeth's 'A little water clears us of this deed' dramatically ironic? Certainly odd, in that it follows hard on Macbeth's admission that all great Neptune's multitudinous seas will not wash the blood from his hand. One would expect to meet these statements in the opposite order, the profound metaphorical one supplanting the literal and superficial. But Macbeth speaks while his wife is away gilding the faces of the grooms. And—the juxtaposition still showing the disparity in imagination between the two of them—the scene needs to end briskly since someone is knocking at the gate.

We may be tempted to read *Measure for Measure* as similarly ironic *in toto*, but, however devoutly we may wish it, we shall fail in the event, and have to rest content with local ironies of an obvious sort. ' 'Tis one thing to be tempted,' Angelo declares,

'Another thing to fall.' In the next scene he is tempted and prepares to fall at the earliest opportunity. Having dismissed the feeble ruse of unloading the guilt on the tempter (who in this case doesn't mean to tempt) rather than the tempted, he comes up with the paradoxical thought that foul desire is most provoked by fair virtue:

> O cunning enemy that, to catch a saint,
> With saints dost bait thy hook . . .

(Or, like Timon of Athens, Isabella is to be brought low by her own heart, 'undone by goodness'.) At this juncture Angelo seems quite unironical in counting himself among the saints, we note; unless he is simply playing on his own name. He is still blaming the tempter, now figuring as some indeterminate 'cunning enemy'.

A more powerful counter-irony was manifest earlier in the same scene, in that great speech of Isabella's which, if it doesn't justify the play's existence, justifies hers. It goes some way to defusing Mephistopheles' disingenuous astonishment over the Crucifixion:

> Why, all the souls that were were forfeit once,
> And He that might the vantage best have took
> Found out the remedy.

This has the ring of something really meant by the author. In comparison, 'More than our brother is our chastity', though addressed to herself, sounds like a party leader in the House of Commons; and 'I had rather my brother die by the law than my son should be unlawfully born' like a sententious family lawyer's attempt at wit.

*

Where extractable ironies are concerned, the richest source in Shakespeare is Prince Hamlet, which fact could be seen as supporting the theory that irony is a substitute for action. Apart from muttered asides ('A little more than kin, and less than kind'), his ironies can be assigned to five main groups.

1. Those exchanged with Horatio, in the relatively jocular spirit of a fellow student: has Horatio come to see Hamlet's father's funeral—or was it to see his mother's wedding? Or both, since the funeral baked meats served as a cold collation for the marriage tables?

2. The mocking hostility shown towards Polonius (who at least recognized method in Hamlet's madness): rather tedious except when he puts him right on the question of using people after their desert.

3. The self-punishing ironies: 'What's Hecuba to him, or he to Hecuba?' The travelling player grieves passionately for a fictitious death while Hamlet mopes silently over his own father's murder; the sense of default is intensified by the sight of the Norwegian army on its way to fight for a patch of land 'which is not tomb enough and continent / To hide the slain', yet twenty thousand men are ready to die for it while he, with more cause for action, remains idle.

4. The cruel treatment of Ophelia (in which there must surely be further self-laceration), who thinks that beauty and honesty go well together, a view not held or at least not practised by his mother, and who tactlessly offers to put him right on a point of chronology, apparently not his forte:

What should a man do but be merry? For, look you, how cheerfully my mother looks, and my father died within's two hours.

Nay, 'tis twice two months, my lord.

So long? Nay, then, let the devil wear black, for I'll have a suit of sables. O heavens! Die two months ago, and not forgotten yet?

5. The generalized ironies of the churchyard scene, in the old tradition of the grave's democracy: Lord Such-a-one's skull is now Lady Worm's, and Alexander's dust stops up the bung-hole in a beer-barrel; 'Here's fine revolution, an we had the trick to see't.'

Then of course there is the affair of Guildenstern and Rosencrantz, who in assiduously working for Hamlet's death ('making love' to the job, as he puts it) bring about their own. To have 'the enginer hoist with his own petar', that prime expression of our subject, is sport indeed! Less satisfying, in the circumstances, is Laertes' death by his own poisoned rapier. A variation on the theme was voiced by Hamlet, just before the fencing began, in his apology to Laertes:

> Let my disclaiming from a purpos'd evil
> Free me so far in your most generous thoughts,
> That I have shot mine arrow o'er the house,
> And hurt my brother.

(The First Folio compositor's 'mother' was either a Freudian slip or an indication of his view of the play's significance.)

*

'Satisfying' isn't quite the term one would apply to the not uncommon modern phenomenon of terrorists—freedom fighters, as it may be, on their way to take liberties with other people—hoisting themselves with their own explosives. Even less would one care to use it of the superficially similar incident in Franz Werfel's documentary novel, *The Forty Days of Musa Dagh* (1933), when the Turks suffer an outbreak of typhus originating with the masses of Armenian corpses in the Mesopotamian deserts. No man is a sanitized island, every man's death diminishes even his enemies, and so forth. But one guesses that the chief 'enginers' of the Armenian massacres were not to be found among the victims of the epidemic, and that many innocent Turks were. This particular irony, promising to enforce a good, humane principle, even if only—remembering Macbeth's 'poison'd chalice' transferred to his own lips—through fear or prudence, quickly loses its flavour. Saddest of all is the irony that flops because its price is too high.

Swift, Fielding, and Bad Taste

IRONY, wrote Swift, ignoring the claims of Socrates—

> Which I was born to introduce,
> Refin'd it first, and shew'd its use.

So we can scarcely not say something about him, even though everything has been said already.

Man is not truly a rational animal, Swift told Pope, but rather an animal capable of reasoning. His Modest Proposer is eminently so capable; the case he makes out for the utilization of poor Irish infants as comestibles is watertight in every particular. They would only grow up to be thieves or else 'leave their dear native country, to fight for the Pretender in Spain'. There are of course the preventive expedients of abortion or infanticide, but these are monstrous measures and 'would move tears and pity in the most savage and inhuman breast'. The impeccable logic is reinforced by sound arithmetic: if you subtract those offspring who miscarry or die by accident or disease within their first year and also those (a small number, sad to say) whose parents can afford to support them, and then allow for those needed for breeding purposes, you are left with 100,000 per annum—a steady but not inconveniently excessive supply.

There can be no disputing that a well-nursed child, at one year old, makes delicious, nourishing, and wholesome eating, however prepared.* (Preferable by far to crocodile meat. The

---

*Though it is said that in thirteenth-century Egypt the flesh of physicians was favoured by all classes. Seized with the pangs of hunger, a man would make out that he was sick and call in a doctor, not to seek his advice but to eat him.

argument is grounded in the fact that we do eat, and find delicious and nourishing, the flesh of lambs and calves.) Further computation shows that one child will make two dishes 'at an entertainment for friends' (we are decent, cultivated people, we have friends, we treat them generously) and, unlike some foods, the commodity will be in season throughout the year, though more plentiful around the month of March. (Oh? Ah yes, June marriages are popular, considered lucky because Juno is the protectress of marriage and of women.) No mean economist, the proposer is quick to work out the profit margin for all (or virtually all) concerned; an incidental asset is the skin, which can be used to make, not necessarily lampshades, but certainly ladies' gloves.

Then there come, not least, the moral advantages. The scheme will be a powerful inducement to marriage and the proper care of babies, and also to the better treatment of pregnant women since husbands will think twice before kicking them and possibly causing a miscarriage. (The implication, pretty well hidden under the savoury smell of cooking, is—as Leavis put it—'This is the only kind of argument that appeals to you; here are your actual faith and morals. How, on consideration, do you like the smell of them?') Moreover, the advocate has done his homework as regards the political implications: the commodity won't bear exportation, being of 'too tender a consistence' to last long in salt, and hence there will be no risk of disobliging England or any other member of the Common Market.

Admittedly, there are, as there always have been, more ways than one of skinning a cat. The condition of the poor could be alleviated if absentee landlords were taxed, if local manufactures were bought instead of imported goods whenever possible, if luxuries were renounced, if people could learn to love their country . . . But it would be absurd to imagine that these remedies will ever be put into practice. In conclusion, for if a proposal is to win universal acceptance the sponsor must be seen to have no vested interest, the writer makes it clear that his own children are grown up and his wife is past child-bearing.

This is the strongest, most sustained irony, where the exposition is so persuasive, the tone so dispassionate and 'objective', the practical benefits so modestly laid out and the anticipated objections so honestly faced, that even the informed reader can hardly forbear to nod his head in assent (if only the scheme had been available to that Chinese mother!) and needs to remind himself of what the proposer is actually proposing.*

The writer twisted the knife, so to speak, by observing that infants' flesh could feature aptly on the menu at convivial gatherings, 'particularly weddings and christenings'. Christopher Hitchens recently reported that *A Modest Proposal* had been banned by a school board in New York State on the grounds that it was 'in bad taste'. (Bad taste would indeed constitute an objection to cannibalism, but our fears on that score have been dispelled.) Possibly what the school board had specifically in mind was the embarrassing reference to 'those voluntary abortions . . . alas! too frequent among us'; yet surely this would have left their charges' withers relatively unwrung? The irony arising out of this banning (not to mention the stupidity) is such that any author of fiction would reject out of hand as beyond the bounds of credibility. Malcolm Muggeridge couldn't have had anything as egregious in view when he wrote that good taste and humour are a contradiction in terms, 'like a chaste whore'.

On second thoughts, it says something for the standard of education in New York State that measures were needed to protect schoolchildren against Swift's indelicacies.

*

The other great classic case concerns the postilion in *Joseph Andrews* who gave his only coat to the robbed and beaten Joseph as the latter lay naked in the snow. The coachman and the passengers all came up with sound and abundant reasons why they should pass quietly by — the man might die on them, he had no

---

*In defending himself against charges of exaggeration, De Quincey adopted a different view. Swift's proposed cannibalism was obviously an extravaganza, whereas 'on the other hand, the tendency to a critical or aesthetic valuation of fires and murders is universal': i.e. *he* hadn't gone too far.

money for the fare, his indecent condition would shock the females, they would feel the cold if they lent him their clothing . . . Here is another modest proposal—this time for doing nothing.

The sharper irony comes in a footnote to the effect that the post-boy—that combination of Good Samaritan and St Martin—was later transported to a penal colony for robbing a hen-roost. The figures of Joseph and the post-boy re-emerge in conflation nearly two hundred years afterwards, in the person of Lem Pitkin of Nathanael West's *A Cool Million* (1934). Lem is wrongly accused of stealing a diamond ring, and beaten unconscious by policemen while awaiting trial. After the verdict of guilty has been brought in, everyone is kind to him, including the officers who had earlier treated him brutally: 'It was through their recommendations, based on what they called his willingness to co-operate, that he received only fifteen years in the penitentiary.'

In an essay on *Tom Jones*, Empson sketches a distinction between 'single irony' and 'double irony'. In the former, 'the ironist (A) is fooling a tyrant (B) while appealing to the judgement of a person addressed (C)', whereas in 'double irony' 'A shows both B and C that he understands both their positions'; characteristically B holds 'the more official or straight-faced belief', and presumably A hopes that both B and C will think 'He is secretly on my side, and only pretends to sympathize with the other', though he may actually hold a wise balance between them or else be feeling 'a plague on both your houses'.

Empson later cites what seems to him 'a particularly massive bit of double irony, worthy to outlast the imperial eagle of the House of Austria'. Mrs Waters, whom Tom has saved from a fate equivalent to death and who has lost the upper part of her clothing, firmly declines the loan of his coat—'I know not for what reason,' says the author. Empson adduces three reasons: Mrs Waters wanted to look pathetic; she wanted to let her comely young saviour see her breasts, her best feature; she honestly didn't want him to take off his coat on such a cold night.

78

(Actually it was early in the morning, but this doesn't make any difference except perhaps that her pathetic expression, or her breasts, would be seen more clearly.) Much taken with Tom, Mrs Waters gathers that he is in love with some younger woman, but she doesn't let this consideration—or the fact that she is old enough to be his mother—stand in her way.

She could feast heartily at the table of love, without reflecting that some other already had been, or hereafter might be, feasted with the same repast: a sentiment which, if it deals but little in refinement, deals, however, much in substance; and is less capricious, and perhaps less ill-natured and selfish, than the desires of those females who can be contented enough to abstain from the possession of their lovers, provided they are sufficiently satisfied that no one else possesses them.

It is this that strikes Empson as a massive piece of double irony, 'though I take it Fielding just believed what he said, and only knew at the back of his mind that the kind of man who would otherwise complain about it would presume it was irony'. I would judge that Fielding more than 'just' believed what he said, especially the part relating to those other females. To some readers this may have proved disconcerting or even scandalous, an up-ending of the decent, accepted view of things, but I cannot believe that the reader who was going to complain about the slur on respectable virgins would be dissuaded from doing so because he supposed the author was being ironic. If he was that sharp, would he be that stupid?

Empson is exceptionally agile, but his manœuvres at this point demonstrate again how tricky it can be to unwind ironies; sometimes one can't see the mist for one's own breath. Fielding is famous for irony, but there are more ways than one of catching your readers on the hop; and one of them is to speak frankly and plainly.

Pope, Grass, and Dogs

'A BEING darkly wise, and rudely great', 'Great lord of all things, yet a prey to all', 'Born but to die, and reas'ning but to err', 'The glory, jest, and riddle of the world!' Here, bleakly mapped, is the ground from which ironies spring in their myriads.

Pope is the master of the one-liner, tapping in the pin as deftly as a connoisseur transfixing a butterfly. 'The smiles of harlots, and the tears of heirs'; 'Or give th' hysteric or poetic fit'; 'And sleepless lovers, just at twelve, awake'.* This is the wit of juxtaposition—'Juxtaposition is great', said Clough, or his character Claude, 'but, you tell me, affinity greater'—or the discovery of occult (and shaming) resemblances in things apparently (or officially) unlike: more effective in implication, because more casual-seeming, more (you might say) 'natural', than the productions of the surrealists, where things are more often yoked together by accident or whim. Thus, 'Or lose her heart, or necklace, at a ball', 'Or stain her honour, or her new brocade', and, of the litter on Belinda's dressing-table, 'Puffs, powders, patches, bibles, billet-doux'.

Pope's lines can be less like the lepidopterist's pins and more like nails hit on the head with some measure, at least, of that energy deriving from the strong antipathy of good to bad. As in

> The hungry judges soon the sentence sign,
> And wretches hang that jurymen may dine

(cf. Seamus Heaney's half-liner in 'Funeral Rites': 'each neigh-

---

*Some wet blanket has argued that agitated lovers, awake all through the night, might excusably fall asleep in the morning.

bourly murder'), or, moving from *The Rape of the Lock* to *Moral Essays, Epistle III*, in that plausible, mild-mannered question,

> And if we count among the needs of life
> Another's toil, why not another's wife?

A low-pressure irony of expectation thwarted occurs in an otherwise lame little poem, not even successfully banal, about lying in the Earl of Rochester's bed at Adderbury:

> With no poetic ardours fir'd,
> I press the bed where Wilmot lay:
> That here he lov'd, or here expir'd,
> Begets no numbers grave or gay . . .

The words 'lying' and later 'lie' ('such thoughts, as prompt the brave to lie . . .') make one wonder whether Pope is telling the truth, for between them love and death ought to generate something a little less unsensational than this. Perhaps he simply slept well.

Death and perhaps love (inconspicuous by its temperance) feature in the most brilliant of Pope's collocations in the mode of *discordia concors* (Johnson's terminology again):

> Not louder shrieks to pitying heav'n are cast,
> When husbands or when lapdogs breathe their last.

Yet we may harbour doubts about the seriousness or sincerity of its satire. Husbands, as distinct from beaux, play no further part in *The Rape of the Lock*; and Pope was to note in the *Essay on Man** that God 'sees with equal eye . . . a hero perish, or a sparrow fall', and to add, apropos of our tendency to complain about heaven failing to devote its full care and attention to us, that his reader, 'wiser' than the untutored Indian who expects his faithful dog to accompany him to a humbler sort of heaven, will

---

*Starting a fresh irony, John Carey has asked how Pope, who had spent half a lifetime writing satire, could take seriously a philosophic poem urging, as its world view, that 'Whatever is, is right'.

Destroy all creatures for thy sport or gust,
Yet cry, If man's unhappy, God's unjust.

*

Dogs, seemingly about to breathe their last, come off well in Günter Grass's novel, *Local Anaesthetic* (1970), certainly better than husbands. During the Vietnam war, young Scherbaum proposes to bring home the horrors of napalm by dousing his pet dachshund with petrol and setting fire to it in front of the cake-consuming ladies in Kempinski's. Enlightenment by demonstration, he calls it. Incinerating himself wouldn't work. You could raise a cross on Kurfürstendamm and crucify Christ during the rush hour, and people would gather to watch, push and shove for a better view, and take pictures if they had their cameras on them,

but if they see somebody burning a dog, burning a dog in Berlin, they'll hit him and go on hitting him until there's not a quiver left in him, and then they'll hit him some more.

Fortunately young Scherbaum's ardour is damped before he can become that most pathetic of things, a martyr to a cause no higher than sloppy thinking.

Northanger Abbey and the Double Take

'. . . but are they all horrid, are you sure they are all horrid?'
'Yes, quite sure; for a particular friend of mine, . . . one of the
sweetest creatures in the world, has read every one of them.' Ah,
days of innocence!

And yet a surfeit of Gothic romances leads Catherine, another
sweet creature, to confuse low literature and upper-class life, and
to believe that General Tilney has either murdered his wife or
immured her in a secret chamber. Of course the General has done
no such un-English thing. How could an atrocity of this nature be
committed without prompt discovery in a country like ours—so
the General's son, Henry, expostulates—'where every man is
surrounded by a neighbourhood of voluntary spies . . .?' (In
some countries an up-to-date version would go: how could bur-
glaries be committed where every house is under surveillance by
state security?) In the event, having driven Catherine out on
finding her less wealthy than he had supposed and ordered Henry
to think of her no more, the General is revealed as a domestic
monster.

Jane Austen being at her most relaxed here, the central irony is
glossed by Catherine herself, who reckons that in suspecting the
General of killing or incarcerating his wife, 'she had scarcely
sinned against his character, or magnified his cruelty'. Her
intuition was right, her reading merely contributed a tinge of
melodrama.

The novel began thus: 'No one who had ever seen Catherine
Morland in her infancy, would have supposed her born to be an
heroine.' We took the tip, or the bait—no young woman with
her genteelly humdrum background could ever be a heroine,

certainly not a girl introduced in this fashion, with such gratifying complicity, by an authoress known for her satirical disposition. And we smiled complacently when, hot on the track of the
missing wife, Catherine comported herself like a romantic
ingénue. Then it turns out that we have been tricked, and in her
humble and quite realistic way Catherine is a bit of a heroine.

The 'double take' is always part of our response to irony, as we
move or are jolted from what was said to what is meant, or, as it
may be, from what we understood to what (we remind ourselves)
we have actually heard. In *Northanger Abbey* this happens on a
large scale, though gently and taking its time. A short, sharp
example, rather like a train steaming determinedly along the
track which, without our noticing it happen, is suddenly seen to
have reversed direction, occurs in *Sense and Sensibility*, when
Robert Ferrars, observed in the protracted act of choosing a
toothpick case for himself, gives the impression of 'a person and
face, of strong, natural, sterling insignificance'.*

An entertaining and rather more intricate specimen comes in a
poem of Dunstan Thompson's entitled 'A Story which I Like',
describing a sumptuous dinner where Flaubert is seated next to
one of the Rothschilds.

> The writer said to his neighbour,
> Over the coffee and Armagnac:
> 'There is a problem which I cannot solve,
> Monsieur le Baron,
> But which perhaps you could explain.'
> 'Of course,' said the great banker, 'If I can.'
> 'Well, then, why do Government stocks go up and down?'
> 'Ah, Monsieur,' replied Rothschild,
> 'If I knew that, I would be a rich man.'

*Cf. Proust, in an early story, 'Un Dîner en ville': 'Her eyes sparkled with stu-
pidity', and Gore Vidal on Harold Acton's volumes of autobiography: 'The ongoing story of a long and marvellously uninteresting life'. In a different class is
James's evocation in *The Bostonians* of Mrs Farrinder, that 'mixture of the
American matron and the public character', who lectures on temperance and
women's rights: 'at almost any time', she 'had the air of being introduced by a few
remarks'.

A triple rather than a double take: (1) we wouldn't expect a person like Flaubert, an artist and a bohemian, to be *au fait* with these matters, but Rothschild will surely understand them; (2) yes, but the activities of the stock market are wrapped in mystery, are even inexplicable, as we learn from financial experts talking on television; (3) but the Baron *is* a rich man!

Probably the double take most remarkable for brevity together with wit, surprise, and shock comes in half a line near the beginning of *Absalom and Achitophel*. Absalom is so outstandingly beautiful and brave among David's numerous progeny that at the moment of his conception his father must have been 'inspir'd by some diviner Lust'.

Hardy Perennial

ONE would suppose that

> some mean, monstrous ironist
> Had built this mistimed fabric of the Spheres
> To watch the throbbings of its captive lives . . .

Such an all-inclusive monolithic *Weltanschauung*, with the Immanent Will busily working its 'eternal artistries in Circumstance', is rather more forgivable in a brainsick student of irony than in a novelist, supposedly the exponent of 'the one bright book of life'.

Hardy provided a neat résumé of basic irony in setting out his intention in *Jude the Obscure*, that wholesale case. It was to display, through the 'grimy' features of the story, a more or less universal and timeless phenomenon, 'to be discovered in *every* body's life', and just a little more clearly exposed to view in his 'poor puppet's': 'the contrast between the ideal life a man wished to lead, and the squalid real life he was fated to lead'. This came in a letter to Edmund Gosse, 10 November 1895. Gosse cannot be blamed for asking none the less, in a review of the novel, 'What has Providence done to Mr Hardy that he should rise up in the arable land of Wessex and shake his fist at his Creator?'

To illustrate the point that irony can be made more striking either by stressing the incongruity of what happens or by stressing the innocence of the person to whom it happens, Muecke suggests that while it was ironic, after all the publicity, that Joanna South-cott did not give birth to the Prince of Peace, 'it would still have been ironical if, with less publicity beforehand and less confidence, she had given birth to the Prince of Darkness instead'. We may suspect that if Hardy had written a novel on the theme, a fair amount of prior publicity and of hopefulness would have ushered in the Prince of Darkness. According to her diary, he told Virginia Woolf that none of his books were fitted to be wedding presents.

Hardy's irony can vary from the heaviest to the lightest; and it is in his poetry that he is writing, even when most seriously, at his lightest. Not invariably so, however. In a poem subtitled 'A Workhouse Irony' a kindly curate has persuaded the Board of Guardians to allow a long-married old couple to live together instead of being assigned to separate wings. The narrator, the husband, is aghast at this news:

> I thought they'd be strangers aroun' me,
>> But she's to be there!
> Let me jump out o' waggon and go back and drown me
>> At Pummery or Ten-Hatches Weir.

Like the curate, the innocent reader anticipates gladness—and gratitude—from him, and prepares to rejoice that the barbaric rule separating husband and wife has been waived. He would be in for a rude shock, were it not that the old man's dismay has been voiced at the outset, and except that the speaker is a cartoon figure in the manner of *Punch* of olden times. No doubt somebody could be unearthed who felt like this, but if irony is to work there must be truth, centrality, and representativeness in the vicinity; it cannot be enforced through the words or actions of a crackpot or a tiny eccentric minority.

A degree of truth and representativeness there is, we may hope, in the heroine of 'The Ruined Maid'. Instead of bemoaning her fallen condition amid the expected tears and blushes while her rosy-cheeked friend from the country waxes righteous, she leaves it to her poor, sad and weary friend to observe how well dressed and spoken she is, how healthy and cheerful and charming. All she needs to do is agree graciously: 'True. One's pretty lively when ruined.' No doubt not every girl gone to the bad is to be discovered in such fine fettle. But we do not feel, as we do with 'The Curate's Kindness', that we are being got at, called upon to raise our hollow little laughs in support of Mr Hardy as he shakes his fist at his Creator. Here Mr Hardy is cocking a snook.

Jamesian

THE treatment dealt out to Mr Leavenworth, in *Roderick Hudson*, is—by Henry James's standards—somewhat crude, but very funny. A widower, he has made his money in borax, in the Middle West, and is travelling in Europe, a place which, apart from its cultural objects, he doesn't think much of. There is far too much liquor in evidence, and 'no cork has ever been drawn at my command'. On his second visit to Roderick's studio he remarks sympathetically of a figure of a *lazzarone* lounging in the sun: 'Something in the style of the Dying Gladiator?' The sculptor informs him, 'Oh no, he's not dying, he's only drunk.'

Mr Leavenworth first called on Roderick to commission a piece for the retreat he is erecting on the banks of the Ohio, which is to house memorials of his wanderings—for 'are we not told that the office of art is second only to that of religion?' What he desires is a representation in white marble of the idea of Intellectual Refinement.

Roderick agrees to take the job on if Miss Blanchard will sit for it. She is something of a painter herself—'She did backs very well, but was a little weak in faces'—but demurs, feeling that the tribute thus implied could be ironic. ('And there was ever afterwards a reflection of her uncertainty in her opinion of Roderick's genius.') However, Mr Leavenworth wants something less life-like—more monumental and impersonal: 'He spoke as if the young woman's charms might compromise the chastity of his conception.' Once he has left, Roderick exclaims, 'His conception be hanged! His conception is sitting on an india-rubber cushion with a pen in her ear and the lists of the stock exchange in her hand.'

While gratified with the general conception of the sculpture in progress, Mr Leavenworth judges that the 'cerebral development' isn't sufficiently emphasized; Intellectual Refinement requires manifest signs of intellect. Protesting that a sculptor isn't like a tailor, making articles to measure, Roderick declares he will destroy the piece. Mr Leavenworth survives the blow; he marries Miss Blanchard and takes her back to his 'retreat' on the banks of the Ohio. It is Roderick who is destroyed, or destroys himself.

*

Despite the narrator's bravely cheerful manner, the clash between art and reality in the story, 'The Real Thing', is a source of unease if not of pain. Shortly after he has been commissioned to illustrate a contemporary novel of high life, he is visited by a distinguished-looking couple who presumably want to have their portraits painted. But Major and Mrs Monarch have lost their money, and what they want is to model for cash. The Major is every inch a gentleman, his wife likewise a lady, and they look askance at the freckled, h-dropping little cockney, Miss Churm, a professional model who can represent everything from a milk-maid to a charming and dangerous Russian princess. Miss Churm is valuable to the artist because she has no 'positive stamp', merely a low talent for imitation. 'Now the drawings you make from *us*,' Mrs Monarch cries triumphantly, 'they look exactly like us.' Which is precisely the trouble.

The artist notes that while Mrs Monarch approved of him as a superior, for he was her employer, she never thought him quite good enough to be an equal. When he draws from the Monarchs, he ends with 'the real thing, but always the same thing', not with the characters he is trying to represent, and he comes near to losing the commission. The incredulous Monarchs see Miss Churm modelling for the fictitious lady and a young Italian, a failed ice-cream vendor, another *lazzarone*, for the fictitious gentleman.

In a squirmingly embarrassing finale, the servants enact the gentry while the gentry play the servants, tidying the studio and washing up the crockery. The artist gives the Monarchs money to go away. They are an admirable, at least a bravely obstinate, couple; but his association with them may have done him permanent professional harm. If so, he is content to pay the price — 'for the memory'. And, I imagine, for the object-lesson: that in art it is the appearance, not the reality, that matters, for the reality you want grows out of appearance.

*

A happier outcome—for, rather like Malvolio, the Monarchs, a royal pair with nothing to rule over, leave us in some discomposure—is that of 'The Birthplace'. The story opens on a happy note, as the deserving Gedges are translated from the town library of Blackport-on-Dwindle, 'all granite, fog and female fiction', to the custodianship of the Great Poet's early home, 'the Mecca of the English-speaking race', a post for which, being refined and cultivated, they are 'just the thing'. That phrase, bringing the Monarchs to mind, may strike a faint chill.

Uneasiness grows when Gedge takes against the doubtfully veracious stories he must lavish on visitors to the Birthplace. The Poet isn't there now—fair enough—but was He ever there? The place is an empty shell, except for the busts and relics (not necessarily of Him) and the period furniture. Gedge tells his wife that they mustn't, for the sake of their immortal souls, tell too many lies. As she sees it, for the sake of their livelihood, they should comply with the legend, even enrich it. ('The morality of women was special—he was getting lights on that.') The look to be worn at the Birthplace was the beatific, not that of a man with whom something had disagreed: Gedge's scrupulousness, his scorn for the visitors who aren't in the least concerned with the reality of the Poet, make themselves felt, and he is warned by the governors to change his ways.

An intelligent American couple who had admired his scepticism but feared for his future pay a second visit. This time they admire his inspirational performance—pointing out the exact spot where the Poet was born, the hearthstone scraped by his tiny feet, the beams of the ceiling which he tried as a boy to jump up and touch—but still fear for his future. Never mind not telling the truth, but isn't he overdoing the fiction? At that moment the emissary returns, surely to turn the poor Gedges out. But no, he brings them congratulations from the governors and, 'in recognition', a doubling of their stipend. 'The receipts, it appears, speak—', Gedge manages to explain to his wife and the waiting Americans, 'Well, volumes. They tell the truth.'

*

It isn't too easy to be certain of James's attitude towards polite society. His serious artists know they must be on their guard against it, that it is radically hostile to their vocation, and yet . . . (Where else, we have to ask, will they find their public?) For one thing, so many of its members talk—whatever they *say*—like James himself. Lord Mellifont, in 'The Private Life', who doesn't exist once he ceases to move in public, is still a power: his romantic legend pales before the reality. Whereas, it must be granted, Clare Vawdrey, 'the greatest (in the opinion of many) of our literary glories', is for us, the readers, of account only when he is in company: writing means someone closeted in his room, head down. More often James makes his high art out of those who cannot themselves achieve it, who have settled—but never happily—for the second-best, who must content themselves (but they never will) with 'the pomp of Ennismore Gardens'.

And, in 'The Lesson of the Master', General Fancourt—the first impression of the young writer, Paul Overt, is that he was distinguished, 'there was no doubt of that, for something he had done, or perhaps even had not done . . . some years before in India'—is neither foolish nor null. As for his daughter, the lovely and intelligent Marian Fancourt . . . 'What is art but a life—if it be real?' she asks. 'I think it's the only one—everything else is so clumsy!' And the young writer, who has spent years abroad, in places seemingly deficient in cultivated society, can only marvel: 'I had no idea there was any one like this!' O brave beau monde that has such creatures in it!

Only the most agile irony—not, assuredly, earnestness—can cope with the theme. The Master in 'The Lesson of the Master' is Henry St George, 'the great misguided novelist' who has produced three fine works and since then only inferior stuff. We can trust Paul Overt's word on this. Still, as St George and his handsome wife drive off in a brougham, they are for him 'an honourable image of success, of the material rewards and the social credit of literature. Such things were not the full measure, but all the same he felt a little proud for literature.' One does want it to count.

It is when he sees that Overt is in love with Marian Fancourt that St George, who recognizes the genuine article in the young man, reads the lesson of the failed master. He looks back on his artistic conscience, 'one's idea, the singleness of one's aim', as though to a woman whom in some dreadful hour of his youth he had loved and abandoned, and who now haunts him reproachfully. (The metaphor of the female Muse is more than ordinarily apt.) Oh, he has everything—apart from the knowledge of having done the best that was in him. Overt remonstrates: but St George leads a full, rich life, he has a wife and fine young sons, currently at Harrow, Oxford, Sandhurst—isn't there something there for art? They have given him subjects, the other replies, but they have taken away the power to use them. 'I've led the life of the world, with my wife and my progeny; the clumsy, expensive, materialized, brutalized, Philistine, snobbish life of London.'

Paul should study him well—either he can do like him, and have a carriage, a house in the country, a handsome wife, and 'a heart with as many aches', or he can do otherwise, and (though who can be sure of these things?) be a true writer. (All the same, the reader wonders whether so intelligent a man, one with what Paul terms 'a genius for torment', a genius for unsparing and unselfpitying self-analysis, can truly have missed the first-rate.) As for Marian Fancourt, for all her feeling for literature ('She's life herself and she takes a rare interest in imitations'), after a year or so—there would be children, there would be a home—she would sink 'the idea of perfection'. Hoping against hope for the best of two worlds, Paul asks: then can the artist 'produce his effect' only by renouncing happiness? Oh, St George replies, he is not defending art. (To Paul he doesn't have to.) Art is 'an incurable corruption' in an otherwise healthy society: 'Assuredly, the artist is in a false position.' It occurs to us that by comparison 'Tonio Kröger', Thomas Mann's tale of art v. life, creative sickness v. rude health, is if not a crude at any rate a more programmatic, explicit or (dare I use the word?) overt replay, fifteen years later, of this tremendous scene of James's.*

On his return from abroad two years later, Paul discovers that Mrs St George has died in the interim and St George is about to marry Miss Fancourt. Though *he* didn't ('Am I a dupe?'), we could see this coming; but we see that it had to come. For St George has nothing to lose by the marriage and some certain pleasures to gain; he might as well make the most in life of his disgrace in art. What we couldn't have anticipated is the nature of the meeting between the two, the bitter young man, with art's exigencies in front of him, and the older man, with more domestic bliss in prospect but nothing else. 'Are you marrying Miss Fancourt to save me?' 'Not absolutely, but it adds to the pleasure. I shall be the making of you.' But ah, if only he could have saved himself—everything he says impels us to the wish—if only he could have been 'made' by meeting a master at the right time!

Paul leaves, hugging the wrong done to him. How unbearable it will be if in a year or so the man comes out with something approaching his early quality, even finer perhaps than his finest! The only sort of revenge he can hope for is to produce something strong himself. When his new book appears, Mr and Mrs St George, we are told, find it 'really magnificent'. So far St George has published nothing more, but Paul doesn't yet feel safe. The

---

*Mann originally thought of giving his story 'the ugly but thrilling title "Literature". *Illae* lacrimae!' (letter to Heinrich Mann, 13 February 1901).

author—one of those very few who can create authentic authors —has the last word:

I may say for him, however, that if this event were to befall he would really be the very first to appreciate it: which is perhaps a proof that St George was essentially right and that Nature dedicated him to intellectual, not to personal passion.

Too complex and delicate in its ironies for effective paraphrase or précis, James's story has a twist of its own: the near-tragedy— the double near-tragedy—which is its subject emerges, through its style of expression, in the guise of a quite delightful social comedy. Set in drawing-rooms and at dining-tables . . . No breast-beating, no fierce invective, no grand asseverations . . . The only person who remotely threatens to disturb the beautiful urbanity of its art is the young artist, and the person who holds it steady is the failed artist. There must have been something to be said for the materialized, brutalized, and Philistine world of London. Just as, for Thomas Mann, there was much to be said for the burgher and mercantile world of Lübeck.

*

The saddest of James's stories, 'The Beast in the Jungle', is not about art, but might be fancied to be about an artist *manqué*. It is of course ironic in that fairly plainly there is to be no beast. (The abysses, we have been told in another context, 'are all so shallow'.) But the tale doubles back on itself, and there is indeed a beast, a less glamorously terrible one, more like the dead weight of a stuffed tiger, but in its way rapacious enough. And there is, at a crucial moment, an absence of irony where irony ought to have been.

John Marcher lives in the knowledge that 'something or other lay in wait for him, amid the twists and the turns of the months and the years, like a crouching beast in the jungle'. What form this fate of his will take he doesn't know, but clearly his condition is not one he could invite a woman to share. Neither is it a topic he can discuss with people in the normal course of social life. But by some blessing he does find someone he can talk to about this 'distinction' of his, this 'sense of being kept for something rare and strange, possibly prodigious and terrible', and he talks and talks as the months and the years twist and turn and pass. May Bartram asks him at one point whether the great and perhaps annihilating thing that is to happen could possibly be falling in love—for that is how some people see it. Some people perhaps, but not Marcher; he has been in love, and it wasn't overwhelming. He pays scant attention to her comment: 'Then it hasn't been love.'

May Bartram is the only one to know his secret, and the right one. She even seems to know what shape his 'doom' will take, but she won't tell him: it couldn't be talked of 'from this side'. She says, and she hopes, that he may not himself ever be aware of it. She dies—the years have taken their toll—and he is miserable, for he has lost his companion, his support, his fellow watcher in the jungle. Only when he sees in the cemetery a mourner—a fellow mourner, he would say, were it not that the other man is an 'image of scarred passion'—does the desolating realization come to him that he has not lived, he has not loved. May had lived, for she loved him for himself; he had only used her, valued her as the servant of his egotism. She had done all she decently could to save him. But he has met the thing he had been marked out for: to be 'the man of his time, *the* man, to whom nothing on earth was to have happened'. (In comparison, Henry St George's doom savours of the de luxe; he fairly soon knew the nature of his domesticated beast.) It is now, in the jungle—or the desert—of his life, that the beast springs.

Long before, when Marcher acquainted May with his special fate or privilege, he mused that 'if she didn't take the ironic view she clearly took the sympathetic'. Ah that she had taken, and imparted, the ironic view! There would have been no unhappiness, no waste, no jungle, no beast. And no story. Very nearly we wish there had been no story. Only the irony—far from cheap, an expensive one, in no way melodramatic, yet implacable—makes it just about bearable.

Proustian

ON examination, ironies, or what look much like them, are ubiquitous in *Remembrance of Things Past*, but they are so much part of an extended body of speculation and interrogation that they go largely unnoticed as such. That's life, we tell ourselves; or would if we stopped to tell ourselves anything. Or, there's nowt so queer as folk, and Proust's in particular. Proust does not impose his ironies or emboss them; they seep out of a character's tone, his or her idiom of speech, gesture, behaviour, and reaction; they are present in the kind of mimesis which requires no 'speech-over' or running commentary. We assimilate both the fine sentiment stated and the meanness betrayed, the perfunctory, oblique reference or the silent response and the rooted sorrow or longing beneath.

But we can hardly fail to note and to interpret as a comment on high society (though not high society alone) the incident in which the Duc de Guermantes, his heart set on attending a ball, dismisses the report of his cousin's death as an exaggeration. And similarly Baron de Charlus's adoption of a tailor's daughter, whom he graces with one of the family titles at his disposal and then marries to a young nobleman. She dies a few weeks afterwards, and 'the death of a simple little seamstress plunges all the princely families of Europe into mourning'. (Nothing in her life became her like the leaving it.) That the young husband is, or is rumoured to be, an invert is neither here nor there, given Proust. A lighter, explicit reflection on modishness occurs when the narrator comments, apropos of the Duke wearing his 'smoking' at a café-concert, that 'in France we give to everything that is more or less British the one name that it happens not to bear in England'.*

A gentler humour suffuses the figure of aunt Léonie, who took to her bed after the death of her husband, Octave. By degrees her visitors are reduced to very few since she declines to see both those who tell her briskly that a walk in the fresh air would do her good and those who take her account of her condition seriously and murmur the pious hope that, even so, she may still last a while yet. 'In short, my aunt demanded that whoever came to see her must at one and the same time approve of her way of life, commiserate with her in her sufferings, and assure her of ultimate recovery.' Marcel once hears her saying to herself, after wakening from a nightmare: 'God be praised! we have nothing to worry us here but the kitchen-maid's baby. And I've been dreaming that my poor Octave had come back to life and was trying to make me take a walk every day!'

Françoise is presented in much the same way, though a shade more astringently. It is while she is employed as aunt Léonie's cook that the kitchen-maid, who has just given birth, is seized with acute pains at night. Françoise reckons that this is mere malingering, the girl wants to 'play the mistress'. However, having anticipated the after-pains, the doctor had referred the family to certain pages in their medical dictionary which described what could be done by way of first aid. Françoise is sent to fetch the book but fails to reappear. An hour later she is discovered sobbing violently over the symptoms ascribed to a fictitious patient—'Is it possible that God wishes a wretched human creature to suffer so? Oh, the poor girl!'—and oblivious to the real-life poor girl groaning upstairs. Presence makes the heart grow harder; the sufferings of the kitchen-maid only provoke the comment that she must have known what she was doing and no doubt she enjoyed it well enough at the time.

It is the subject of love that generates the majority of Proust's ironies. That Charlus should despise effeminates and worship

*The converse was noted by Stendhal in *De l'amour*: 'The most serious writers in England think they are being dashing by using French words which for the most part were never French except in English grammar-books.'

virile, 'manly' men, even though his love life is complicated as a result, should cause us no astonishment; it is, one could say, only natural. But comedy of a kind derives from his taste for being reviled and whipped by brutal blackguards. The supposed thugs, thieves, pimps and murderers he hires for this purpose are more or less respectable family men, glad to earn a little easy money, and Charlus has some difficulty in sustaining his self-deception.

*

This incident brings to mind a strange tale by Yukio Mishima, a master of the perverse even among Japanese masters. The handsome young couple of 'Three Million Yen' have worked up a modestly rewarding partnership as 'performers' specializing in entertaining rich and bored middle-aged housewives. Unlike some who engage in this business—'exhibition' used to be the word for it—they never fail to give satisfaction. And this is because they never fail to gain satisfaction: they are truly in love, they perform their act with conviction. In fact they are a respectable married couple, their way of life based on faith in the future (not so common in post-war Japan), connubial love, and rational planning. Despising the improvidence of the poor, they are ensuring that when they have the baby they desire the child shall lack for nothing from the start.

Being rational—or, perhaps, being in love—the couple see nothing degrading in their activities. How nice to be paid for doing what you would gladly do for free! True, the man finds their clientele affected and stuck-up, and inveighs against them on the way home for throwing around money they have pried from their husbands. The girl, a born housewife and disinclined to expend energy on unproductive emotion, stays cool: 'The pay was good.'

*

At the end of his tormented passion for Odette, Swann exclaims to himself, 'To think that I've wasted years of my life, that I've longed to die, that I've experienced my greatest love, for a woman who didn't appeal to me, who wasn't even my type!' The narrator attributes this outburst to an old, intermittent caddishness that evinced itself in Swann 'when he was no longer unhappy and his moral standards dropped accordingly'. Here, plainly, is the kind of irony operative when the generally accepted, the received idea, is stood on its head, and so discreetly that we might almost not notice. For we have supposed that caddishness stems from some form of unhappiness, or certainly not from happiness, and that though morality may not necessarily be created by happiness, at any rate unhappiness offers it less opportunity to thrive. We are to find that in *Remembrance of Things Past* happiness is a much lesser thing, in all its side-effects and therefore in itself, than unhappiness. The effects of unhappiness—for 'side-' suggests a false distinction—are sufficiently diverse and documented for us to forget, or simply remain oblivious to, the initial postulate—and hence its supposed irony too. Unhappiness is merely the air these people breathe.

Saint-Loup suffers through his love (one word must stand for so many conditions) for the actress Rachel, whom a few years earlier Marcel could have enjoyed on the cheap in a brothel 'of inferior grade'. Saint-Loup 'had given more than a million francs in order to have, in order that others should not have, what had been offered to me, as to all and sundry, for twenty'. A cheap and brutish irony? When Marcel remarks that, looking at Rachel, though it was the same face they saw, Robert and he did not see her 'from the same side of the mystery', he is demonstrating in exemplary form the circumstances in which irony can commonly arise; but he is also softening the cheap and brutish irony cited. (In an early sketch the young Proust was more dismissive, more banal, and more snobbish, when observing that poets who have created imperishable mistresses often knew nothing better themselves than commonplace barmaids.) Marcel had given the girl the nickname 'Rachel when from the Lord', after a famous aria of the time, and though the madam at the brothel didn't recognize the allusion, she always laughed over it and adopted it herself:

99

'failing to understand a joke has never yet made anyone find it less amusing'. The same can't be said for irony.

*

Much less amusing are the narrator's direct pronouncements on love and its attributes, concomitants and effects.

It is moreover the property of love to make us at once more distrustful and more credulous, to make us suspect the loved one, more readily than we should suspect anyone else, and be convinced more easily by her denials

—to which is added, 'It is human to seek out what hurts us and then at once to seek to get rid of it.' While acknowledging that there is generally something left to 'conquer', we may agree, if uneasily, that

Love, in the pain of anxiety as in the bliss of desire, is a demand for a whole. It is born, and it survives, only if some part remains for it to conquer. We love only what we do not wholly possess.

This is much less warm-hearted than Donne following up his complaint, 'If yet I have not all thy love, / Dear, I shall never have it all', with the second thought, 'Yet I would not have all yet, / He that hath all can have no more.' Even less can one 'wholly possess' the dead. And we might perceive a Metaphysical-type ingenuity or perversion in what Proust proposes some four hundred pages onwards. When our mistress is alive, she is more often than not absent from our side, and no more than a memory, and it is then that the larger part of the thoughts that make up what is called 'love' come to us. We acquire the habit of musing on an absentee. 'Hence death'— the death of the loved one, that is—'does not make any great difference.'

Marcel reports that during the year following Albertine's death he was fully occupied in a love affair with someone who was dead. In the main, it must be said, this 'veritable liaison' consisted in an obsessive and ghoulish investigation—self-protective? self-punishing?—into the poor woman's possible misdeeds. As health is known and measured by sickness, so—it would appear—love is known and measured by jealousy.

Illusion and delusion are ever-present hazards; we are dogged by misunderstanding of people and events, by—an alarming extrapolation!—a 'perpetual error, which is precisely "life" '. Proust's dicta resemble proverbs in that, while they are all in varying degrees persuasive, some of them are contradicted or modified by others; they are akin to Imlac's inconsistencies, which cannot all be right but, where humans are concerned, can all be true. Even so, whatever extenuations and special pleas can be marshalled, on the subject of love Proust is chilling. (We feel a good deal of fond nostalgia for Mme Leroi and her reply, in *The Guermantes Way*, when asked for her views on that subject: 'I make it often but I never talk about it.') Love means pain, and pain is good for the writer. 'The work in which our unhappiness has collaborated may be interpreted both as an ominous sign of suffering and as an auspicious sign of consolation.' As for happiness (bad for our manners? bad for our morals?), well, it has its uses since had we not been happy, if only in hope, 'the unhappinesses that befall us would be without cruelty and therefore without fruit'. For our knowledge of the splendours and miseries of the writer we are dependent on writers. Not for the first time, we wonder what consolations and what fruits fall to those who happen not to be engaged in the literary arts.

*

'. . . since the true paradises are the paradises that we have lost.' Yes, the paradises one possesses usually have a snake or two lurking in the grass; and only a lost love is impervious to change and corruption, or safe from loss. The only perfect life is over— and was, in all probability, rather brief. ('In short measures, life may perfect be.') While the saying about paradises resonates in the imagination, its truth is a petty and senseless one, owing its power to human perversity, to (as it may be) that desire for the better which destroys the good we have. The breezy pronouncement, 'Ah, but a man's reach should exceed his grasp, or what's a heaven for?', is open to much sorrowful emendation.

However persuasive we may find Proust as psychologist—subtle-souled, though at times we have misgivings about his soul—and as moralist, a part of us still resists the will to pain in his writing. It doesn't, we murmur, as almost spellbound we watch Marcel and Albertine, Swann and Odette, Charlus, Saint-Loup, it doesn't *have* to be like that.

Freud and the Conservation of Energy

FREUD was one of the most assiduous of 'significance-seeking organisms', reasonable in supposing that every accident has a cause, ready in discovering exciting causes spiced with 'emotional flavouring'.

Sometimes, if we forget a name, we have a hidden reason, not necessarily very well hidden, for doing so: we wish the owner of it were dead, or had never been born. At other times we forget because we must, as Matthew Arnold has it, and not because we will; because we have a bad memory, or something else is occupying it. Freud will have none of this fudging, or not much. In *The Psychopathology of Everyday Life* (1901), examining parapraxes (slips of the tongue or pen) and 'symptomatic acts', he maintains that 'If we give way to the view that a part of our psychical functioning cannot be explained by purposive ideas, we are failing to appreciate the extent of determination in mental life.' It could be that the mental lives of some people are less determined than those of others. He concedes that in simple cases —when words or letters are left out in speaking or writing—the more complicated interpretations find little foothold, but insists that even so *'some* disturbance of intention' has revealed itself, and it is 'a reasonable scientific demand' that rudimentary or trivial slips 'should be judged on the basis of the more clearly marked cases'. Isn't that demanding too much? The awkward dodging to left and to right when two people meet in the street and try to pass is one of those symptomatic acts, in this case said to mask an erotic purpose. The last time I engaged in the act, the other person was a large policeman.

Among the examples of parapraxis given by Freud, *Anektode* (*Tod*: death) instead of *Anekdote* could happen to anybody, especially if German, though as it happened the anecdote being committed to paper on the particular occasion concerned the hanging of a gypsy. And despite Freud's view that the slip of the tongue can hardly be other than 'an unintentional parody which is a perseveration of an intended one', the toast 'I call on you to hiccup to the health of our Principal' (*aufzustossen* having supplanted *anzustossen*) could merely suggest that some drinking had been done already. And it seems rash to interpret a young woman's bursting into the consulting room while the analyst is still busy with the preceding patient as a demonstration of the curiosity that in the past had led her into her parents' bedroom. We aren't too surprised by Freud's inability to 'claim that one always makes friends of those to whom one shows the meaning of their symptomatic acts'.

On the other hand we see more than sheer accident in the case of the normally careful woman who had been persuaded against her better judgement to go to a play while still in mourning for her mother, and who arrived at the theatre to discover she had lost the ticket, possibly thrown away along with the tram ticket. And something sinister may well have underlain the behaviour of the young man who, when he had escorted his fiancée back to her parents' house, used to get on a tram to go home and ask the conductress for two tickets. Some months after marrying the girl, he noticed that when collecting her after she had visited her parents, and the two of them were on the tram, he was asking for one ticket only. More blatantly revealing is the case of the young lady who forgot about the final fitting for her wedding dress and had to rush to the dressmaker's late on the eve of the ceremony . . . Particularly when the analyst adds, 'Today she is divorced.'

*

Closer to our theme is *Jokes and their Relation to the Unconscious* (1905), in which Freud reveals himself as a spirited raconteur, notably of Jewish jokes. One of them, he observes, is of much wider application. Pleading dire need, an impoverished fellow borrows money from a prosperous acquaintance. Later the same day the acquaintance sees him in a restaurant, a plate of salmon mayonnaise in front of him. Is *that* what he borrowed the money for? But, the fellow protests, 'If I haven't any money, I *can't* eat salmon mayonnaise, and if I have some money I *mustn't* eat salmon mayonnaise. Well, then, when *am* I to eat salmon mayonnaise?'

Jewish in another sense is Heine's lottery agent and corn-cutter, in *Die Bäder von Lucca*, who ends the story of his relations with Baron Rothschild by remarking that the Baron treated him as an equal, 'quite famillionairely' (*famillionär*), thus working off his resentment at the rich man's condescension while boasting of hobnobbing with him. More formal witticisms cited by Freud—he is really enjoying himself in this work—include Voltaire on Jean-Baptiste Rousseau's *Ode to Posterity*: 'This poem will not reach its destination', and Georg Christoph Lichtenberg who, having quoted Hamlet's 'There are more things in heaven and earth than are dreamt of in your philosophy', added in mock rebuke, 'But also there is much in philosophy that is not to be found in heaven or earth'—a pleasing instance of attacking under the guise of defending.*

*It was Lichtenberg who said, 'The critics instruct us to stay close to nature, and authors read this advice; but they always think it safer to stay close to authors who have stayed close to nature.'

Freud's account of the mechanism of pleasure has it that the maintenance of any psychical inhibition involves the expenditure of psychical energy, and a joke serves to lift the inhibition temporarily: 'it is therefore plausible to suppose that *this yield of pleasure corresponds to the psychical expenditure that is saved*'. Here we seem to be approaching a concept of irony and its mode of operation, but in the first of his two references to irony Freud asserts that what we call 'irony' is no longer a joke.

Yet surely there is irony in the American joke he recounts, of two business men who had made their pile by shady means and reckoned that having their portraits painted by a fashionable artist would help them break into polite society. During a party thrown to launch the paintings the men led a celebrated art critic up to the wall on which they were hung. He studied them for a while, shook his head as if bemused, pointed to the gap between the two pictures, and asked: 'But where's the Saviour?' And in discussing the joke technique of representing something by its opposite, Freud cites the story of the monarch, visiting a hospital, who watched the surgeon keenly as he amputated a leg, crying 'Bravo, bravo, my dear Professor!' from time to time. The surgeon resented the idea that he was performing by royal command, for the monarch's entertainment, but dared not show his feelings. So, when the operation was over, he bowed and enquired, 'Is it Your Majesty's command that I should remove the other leg too?'

If this isn't irony, what is? It must be admitted that as a way of saving psychic energy (or one's face) it relies rather dangerously on the other person's stupidity. And the same is true of the royal personage, on tour, who noticed a man bearing a striking resemblance to his own person. Bidding the man approach, he asked him whether his mother was ever in service at the Palace. He had insulted the man's mother, but what could the poor man do about it? He replied: 'No, Your Highness, but my father was', thus contriving to insult both the Highness's mother and his father, and His Highness into the bargain.

Freud describes this as one of those tendentious jokes (as distinct from 'innocent' ones) which are 'highly suitable for attacks on the great, the dignified and the mighty', people who on other fronts are protected either by our internal inhibitions or by external circumstances, including the certainty of having one's head chopped off on the spot. In his other and longer reference to irony, he admits it as one of the subspecies of the comic and rules that it can be employed only when the other person is prepared to hear the opposite and so is bound to feel an inclination to contradict. That it produces comic pleasure in the hearer is 'probably because it stirs him into a contradictory expenditure of energy which is at once recognized as being unnecessary'. Since pleasure has been said to derive from the saving of energy, it seems paradoxical that it should also come from an enforced and gratuitous wastage of it. Freud's theory of irony as bad economics could rather be seen to account for its power to irritate.

*

Sinking into my own anecdotage . . . The following verses, 'Anecdote from William IV Street', are based on an incident that happened when I was working for Freud's British publishers.

> Entering the publisher's warehouse, a foreign young lady
> Asks for Volume XXIV of The Complete Works of Freud.

> (This being the Index, at last, which directs the reader
> To a wealth of unconscious wants he might else overlook.)

> 'I also desire,' says she, extending an elegant arm,
> 'An image of Jesus Christ approximately this high.'

The incident seemed to me—and still seems—to bear some powerful though indistinct symbolic aura, as if it were one of those 'epiphanies' in which the banal and the supernatural merge to astonish and enlighten us. Yet not a single bosom has returned an echo; public readings of the poem have met with silence, as the listeners await the sequel, the undelivered punch line. Efforts to justify the story on the grounds that it illustrates the human tendency to hedge bets—the young lady invests in two famous but adversary healers—have flopped completely. *Anektode* is the word. There must be an explanation, however deeply concealed, for this vagary of mine. Nice if it could be something more momentous than suppressed desire, a suppressed memory of suppressed desire, for the young lady, glimpsed fleetingly from the rear as she left the premises . . .

Politics

WHEN Laertes and his supporters burst into the castle of Elsinore, Claudius informs him,

> There's such divinity doth hedge a king,
> That treason can but peep to what it would,
> Acts little of his will.

The switch in pronouns may suggest some uncertainty on Claudius's part; his bravery is not in dispute, but he speaks more in hope than in expectation. That treason—occupying much the same position then as terrorism does now—could not succeed was for long official doctrine, linked with the principle of divine right. In the face of Essex's rebellion, Queen Elizabeth was reported to have declared that He who placed her on the throne would keep her there. Sir John Harington's famous couplet throws light on the interplay of divine right and treason and usurpation as it and its ironies unfold in history as in Shakespeare's history plays:

107

Treason doth never prosper: what's the reason?
For if it prosper, none dare call it treason.

Nothing succeeds like success; and whatever is, is (divinely, for as long as it lasts) right. Harington's irony has abiding political point for all that in more recent times—the dwindling of God has been matched by a proliferation of secular politicians—people have been none too ready to acquiesce in 'whatever is'. Divine rights have been democratized, within uncertain limits.

Rights are strange things. People who do not believe in God apparently believe they were bestowed by God. It may even happen that one has to be in the wrong to win any. In certain circumstances, Hannah Arendt pointed out in *The Origins of Totalitarianism* (1951), it is only as an offender against the law that one can gain protection against the law. She was speaking of the condition of the stateless person, the person without a 'condition'. The same man who yesterday had no rights, who was in gaol merely because of his presence in the world or lived under the threat of deportation, might become almost a fully fledged citizen simply by virtue of committing a minor theft. 'He is no longer the scum of the earth but important enough to be informed of all the details of the law under which he will be tried. He has become a respectable person.'

*

To begin with a generalization that will need some trimming: irony is non-political. It is often said, in a tone of accusation, that those who describe themselves as non-political are politically reactionary, at best closet conservatives. And it is true that, with its distrust of big words and large claims, and because of the weight of past experience behind it, the spirit of irony inclines to find a target in radical ideologies. During the revolutionary struggle irony is made welcome for its thrusts at the class enemy, and it thrives along with satire against corsets, pin-stripe suits, clerics, bankers, royal families, judges, policemen, and so forth. Once the revolution is in the saddle, irony gets a prompt and dishonourable discharge.

That modern Tory philosophy offers relatively few opportunities for irony must be because there is so little of it.* Tories do well to keep in mind Josef Skvorecky's observation: 'The only mystery that remains is, why bother to conceal the nakedness of power with a whore's G-string of ideology?' (Even so, they should avoid making a spectacle of themselves, for example through an *Arts* Minister resigning on the grounds that he cannot live in central London on his parliamentary salary of £33,000 p.a.†) Explicitly peace-loving religions fairly easily erupt into violence, and the more talk there is of universal brotherhood, the greater the antipathy if not the hatred in the offing. 'All Faith, they say, is like a jewel,' writes Gavin Ewart, 'but why is it so bloody cruel?'

Irony of a generally unimpressive sort is of course visible in the cut and thrust or shadow-boxing of day-to-day party politics. In his memoir, *Vamp Till Ready* (1982), Roy Fuller remarks that when he was a youngish writer it seemed he could only be ironical about things of which he disapproved ideologically—'right-wing politicians, say'. This cast of mind he describes as ' essentially adolescent', referring (I imagine) to the then poverty of his sense of irony rather than its particular target. During the recent coal strike production workers stopped a national newspaper because

---

*Though a passage not wholly inapposite can be found in 'The Lesson of the Master': '. . . the accomplished Mr Mulliner, editor of the new high-class, lively evening paper which was expected to meet a want felt in circles increasingly conscious that Conservatism must be made amusing, and unconvinced when assured by those of another political colour that it was already amusing enough'. Amenable to interpretation as a more topical anti-Tory irony is Charles Gould's defence of the Gould Concession, in *Nostromo*: 'What is wanted here is law, good faith, order, security. Anyone can declaim about these things, but I pin my faith to material interests. Only let the material interests once get a firm footing, and they are bound to impose the conditions on which alone they can continue to exist. That's how your money-making is justified in the face of lawlessness and disorder . . . A better justice will come afterwards.' Later events in the novel mock the fitness of things as thus conceived by the idealistic speaker.

†But this is a mechanical and priggish gibe. The minister, in harmony with the spirit of the age, was merely pinning his faith to material interests.

they objected to the description of striking miners involved in violence as 'scum'. That one could respect. However, the paper continued not to appear, the workers having struck because they hadn't been paid for the issue they had stopped. This strikes me as a true non-specific irony: a stand on principle expecting pay as usual, altruism claiming compensation, a heroic action sliding smoothly into quotidian self-interest. I dare say, though, that to many right-wingers the incident was merely another case of union bloody-mindedness, and to many left-wingers just another skirmish in the war against the bully-barons of Fleet Street.

Irony's guns face in every direction; it is committedly uncommitted, in its essence anti-political, or anti-ideological, whatever the ideology. Politicians of all shades dislike it rather more than they dislike the opposition parties; it doesn't go in for 'pairing' or other mutual arrangements; it is sneaky.

*

Brecht is a key figure here, Brecht at his best and longest-lasting: as a poet, that is. His cast of mind was strongly ironic from the start. An early manifestation is the verse story of Evelyn Roe, who worked her passage to the Holy Land in the only way open to her, and was then barred from heaven on the grounds that she was a harlot and excluded from hell in that she was holy-minded.

The rise of Nazism inspired numerous ironies, from the quasi-jocular 'Hitler Chorales' ('Now thank we all our God / For sending Hitler to us / . . . He'll make sure that it rains / But nobody gets wet') to 'The Burning of the Books': a writer is shocked to find his books omitted from the list for the bonfire and dashes a letter off to the authorities complaining that they are treating him like a liar. The poem arose out of a specific occasion (1933), but—which is why Brecht is of more than 'historical interest'—is universal and (one suspects) timeless in its pertinence.

Not surprisingly, Brecht's Communist and pro-Soviet poems are devoid of irony. Most of us need something to approve of, especially in the face of something we must reject. (Though

Heine, forced to choose between nationalism and Communism, chose neither.) Reading 'The carpet weavers of Kuyan-Bulak honour Lenin' ('Often and copiously honour has been done / To Comrade Lenin'), we could think we were in a poem by Cavafy and it would soon recoil like a scorpion and sting itself. It doesn't: a pious act is piously recorded, there is no irony in the weavers' decision not to spend money on a bust but to buy the petroleum that will rid them of mosquitoes, and, self-righteously rather than self-defensively, a plaque is put up to make things plain. Even flatter is the celebration of the newly opened Moscow Metro, a unique and specifically Marxist phenomenon, 'the builders in the role of proprietors'. Such poems, one supposes, are of some slight 'historical interest'.

But other 'Communist' poems survive by virtue of their independence from ideology or unique occasions. 'Questions from a worker who reads', for example, with its Socratic irony: 'Philip of Spain wept when his armada / Went down. Was he the only one to weep?' And the poem 'On sterility'—which in typescript was first called 'Stalin's song' and then 'Mao's song'—is simultaneously non-political, anti-political, and highly political, because thoroughly human and humane:

> The branch that breaks
> Is called rotten, but
> Wasn't there snow on it?

Brecht was too much of a pessimist—the minor villain of every radical piece—to make a sound, sincere ideologue. 'Praised be doubt!' one of his poems opens, and doubt is of course commonly expressed through irony, or generated by it. (Even-handedly, he goes on to warn against both 'the thoughtless who never doubt' and 'the thoughtful who never act'.) He was insufficiently romantic in disposition, not enough of an idealist, albeit in some circumstances cynicism or a rapacious egocentricity, with both of which he was well endowed, can stand in for idealism. In his private life and, most patently, in the theatre his attitude resembled that of Heine in political matters: 'We are all

111

brothers, but I am the big brother . . .'* It was right and proper for others to follow *the* Way—and indeed Marxism provided a 'philosophical respectability' (Martin Esslin's phrase) for part at least of his natural and instinctive behaviour—but he wanted his own way, as much as he could get of it, whether by bullying, by guile, or through the exercise of discretion.

As an artist, Brecht was in love with catastrophe; no political or social policy could ever root out the old Adam in humanity, and if by some secular miracle we were offered the Earthly Paradise on a plate we should promptly spill it in the mud. Such scepticism doesn't preclude compassion for the victims of human perversity or viciousness, or discourage attempts at amelioration, but it rules a man out as a party laureate. 'Here you have someone on whom you can't rely' was true of Brecht, and not only in the amatory sphere. The genuine ironist is impartial and implacable; he can't be trusted to blinker himself or bite back words; even what he may consider his better judgement fails to intervene to much effect.

Brecht's most celebrated irony was inspired by the rising in East Germany of 17 June 1953 (though the poem in question wasn't published there until 1964): since the people have forfeited the confidence of the government, isn't the easiest thing for the government to dissolve the people and elect another? It being in the nature of governments to exceed their role, all governments please note.

Whatever Brecht's opinion of Stalin—which did he think him?: the 'great harvest-leader' or the 'meritorious murderer of the people'? or first one and then the other?—in 1955 he accepted

*Where programmes were concerned, both poets were better at fighting against than fighting for. The *Tendenzbär*, the bear with a tendency who is the eponymous hero of Heine's *Atta Troll* (1843), calls for the animals to unite against the tyranny of man and to create a beastdom founded on justice. All shall be equal, any ass can rise to the highest office while a lion may find himself hauling sacks to the mill. Even Jews shall enjoy full civic rights—except that dancing in the streets will be forbidden them. Atta Troll imposes this minor reservation for the sake of the art he himself practises: Jews lack rhythm and would debase public taste. Heine is thought to have had in mind a Göttingen pharmacist who campaigned for rights for Jews—all of them apart from the right to set up as pharmacists.

a Stalin Peace Prize. And deposited the proceeds in a Swiss bank. In the following year the award was renamed the Lenin Peace Prize. Like some other things, prizes can smell sweeter by another name. Like treason, in fact.

*

If nothing succeeds like success, nothing fails like failure. (Though failure isn't always the right word.) In Böll's *Billiards at Half-past Nine*, Schrella—like most of this author's favoured characters — is permanently in the wrong. (Though wrong isn't quite the right word, either.) A refugee from the Nazis, he was imprisoned in Holland for threatening a Dutch politician who contended that all Germans should be killed. When the Germans entered the country they freed him under the impression that he was a national martyr, and then found his name on their list of wanted persons. So he had to escape to England. There he was imprisoned for uttering threats against a British politician who declared that all Germans should be killed and only their works of art preserved. However, he was released on probation, on the grounds that his feelings ought to be respected—feelings he hadn't felt at all when making the threats. 'Thus one gets locked up because of a misunderstanding, and because of a misunderstanding one is set free.'

Censorship

MAYBE Shaw's *bon mot*, that assassination is the extreme form of censorship, goes some way to reconciling us to the latter, especially if we happen to be faced with the choice. Then we recall the less amusing proposition made by a character in Heine's *Almansor* (1823): where people burn books, before long they will burn men also.

*

In *The Element of Irony in English Literature* (1926), F. McD. C. Turner cites as typical of Milton's second-best and most common ironical style (no evidence is offered of his first-best) the passage in *Areopagitica* about the detested word *Imprimatur*. The reason behind this piece of apish Romanizing must be either that 'the learned Grammatical pen that wrote it, would cast no ink without Latin' or else that no vulgar, i.e. modern, tongue was considered worthy 'to express the pure conceit of an *Imprimatur*'. Or—the explanation Milton hopes and suggests is the true one—because English, the language of men ever to the fore in matters of liberty, cannot easily find 'servile letters anow' to spell so tyrannous a word. The climax is certainly a grand one, but . . . Milton knew that the English language contained words signifying rape and murder, let alone censorship and licensing, and we know he knew. Here he seems to be huffing and puffing as if less than habitually confident of the truth of what he is asserting.

A stronger passage, I would say, comes later in the pamphlet, when Milton's temper has subsided. He remarks that those who are to 'sit upon the birth or death of books' will need to be

114

exceptionally able, learned, and knowledgeable men. And he adds quietly that men of such rare worth will find the job of reading an unending stream of 'unchosen books and pamphlets, ofttimes huge volumes' quite unendurable. Thus registering a form of catch-22 which could conceivably be extended to modern book reviewers.*

*

In countries and under regimes where what writers say is of public moment, writers are censored, imprisoned, or silenced in some other way. Where freedom of speech prevails, the writer is usually of little public importance. Another catch-22 situation. At least in the former type of country officially approved writing, however unexciting, sells generously, perhaps because of some persistent respect for books and because boring books are better than none. Good or bad?

In Beaumarchais's *Le Mariage de Figaro*, the hero gathers that a system of press freedom has been instituted whereby, so long as in his writing he mentions neither the authorities, nor religion, nor politics, nor morality, nor the Establishment, nor other people of importance, nor the Opéra, nor other theatrical productions, nor anybody who has something to do with anything, then he is at liberty to print whatever he wishes, under the scrutiny of two or three censors.† (To profit from such sweet freedom, Figaro proposes to found a periodical to be called *Journal inutile*. An echo is heard in Mark Twain's passage on the 'three unspeakably precious things': freedom of speech, freedom of conscience,

---

*My own opinion of reviewers must be slightly higher than Henry James's. In 'The Private Life' the narrator says of an admired author whose conversation lags so far behind his writing that in effect there are two of him, that even so (and given the prodigious Swiss thunderstorm raging at the time), 'It broke my heart to hear a man like Vawdrey talk of reviewers.'

†The catch was repeated by Stendhal in *Le Rouge et le Noir*, in relation to the subjects of conversation allowable *chez* the Marquis de La Mole, and recurs in Lady Utterword's speech in Shaw's *Heartbreak House*: 'I am a woman of the world, Hector; and I can assure you that if you will only take the trouble always to do the perfectly correct thing, and to say the perfectly correct thing, you can do just what you like.'

and the prudence never to practise either of them.) *Le Mariage* was banned, Louis XVI declaring that 'It shall never be played.' But it was, three years later. Louis lost his head some nine years later still, in 1793.

An amusing variant on this came up more recently. A book called *The Malay Dilemma*, written in 1970 by Mohamad Mahathir, was banned in Malaysia as 'racialist'. Ten years later the ban was lifted, a fortnight after the author became Prime Minister of the country. (Too arduous a method of getting one's books distributed to be generally recommended.)

Keeping politics out of poetry, once you have been suspected of putting them in, is quite difficult. Almost as difficult as it is—according to Malcolm Bradbury's Dr Jochum, a European refugee at Benedict University in the United States—to teach political science: 'One has to try so hard to keep politics out of politics.'

My own slight and innocuous experience of the Special Branch —not Britain's Special Branch but one inherited from Britain in good working order—led me to believe that its members had little understanding of irony but a healthy suspicion of it. They could smell it, and hence, perplexed and wary, were not too quick to hustle the handcuffs on. They didn't mind feeling foolish in the privacy of their hearts, but they did not relish being made fools of in public. (It was in this country—if I may be indulged in a tiny irony of my own—that I apparently agreed, in a moment of self-censorship of which I wasn't aware, not to publish anything locally; there were no magazines for which I could have written, which took the sting out of the prohibition.)

Yet it is unwise to rely on fear of ridicule for protection against such attentions. True, when the police in Singapore objected to an amateur production of William Inge's *Picnic*, there was at least the opportunity of discussing their unease with them. It turned out that a reference to enjoying 'a shaker-full of martini' in the back seat of a car was thought to signify a sexual orgy. (Advertising copy there?) Explanations were made and the objection was withdrawn just before the curtain was due to go up.

These things get about—and why risk unkind laughter? In France, during the occupation, the publishers Gallimard submitted the manuscript of Valéry's *Mauvaises Pensées et autres* to the German authorities, as required. It is said that the censor, sadly out of his depth, asked plaintively: 'Why doesn't he write the Good ones?'

On another Singapore occasion, however, a senior policeman who had scrutinized the text of *Sweeney Agonistes*, to be read in public by a university group, objected to the phrase 'birth, and copulation, and death', stating that while he was prepared to allow one 'copulation' he found himself having bad thoughts by its fifth appearance.* Such a fresh response, and so courageous a declaration of it! His word was final, there was no arguing with him, any more than with Brigadier Adly el-Kosheiry, head of the Interior Ministry's delinquents' department in Cairo, when he ruled that because of the dirty words in it the unexpurgated version of *The Thousand and One Nights* was not a classic but a threat to Egyptian youth. In performance Eliot's line had to be changed to 'birth, and procreation, and death'. I don't for a moment believe the policeman's thoughts were any worse than he was used to. He was reading the minds of his more sensitive superiors in the government. Only innocents would consider it odd that the minds of such stout anti-Communists should work in a manner so close to that of the Soviet censor in 1956 who, dissatisfied with the gloomy picture of human life painted in some lines of Pasternak's, 'Amid the earthly circuit of birth, suffering and death', rewrote the final phrase as 'of birth, work and death'. These people—even as we make fun of them, we must grant it—know the magical power of words.

Books tend to fall apart in Singapore's humid atmosphere, and I had the *Collected Poems* containing 'birth, and copulation, and death' re-bound (and very nicely) by the inmates of a local prison. I suppose they were judged not to be great readers, or else immune to further corruption.

Incidentally, the book in which I first recounted these

*Cf. the repetition of the word 'honourable' in Antony's speech.

outbreaks of censorial prurience was itself banned in due course. (Copies that had already reached the shops were sold pre-wrapped from under the counter: the commercial factor isn't always to be deplored.) The ban was lifted a year later, soon after my departure from the country. It looked very much as though—anything ironical here?—the co-presence of the book and its author was more than reasonable liberality could stomach.

*

In a version of Villon's 'Ballade des dames du temps jadis' used in French schools Abelard's fate was euphemized by changing one letter, so that *châtré* (castrated) became *châtié* (punished). In *Don Juan*, however, mention is made of school editions of the classics the editors of which had excised the grosser parts but, reluctant to mutilate the author too badly, 'They only add them all in an appendix, / Which saves in fact the trouble of an index.' 'Fact,' says a footnote, specifying an edition of Martial's epigrams.

The dominant irony in this sphere, of course, is that banning often increases a thousandfold the demand for what is banned and hushing-up results in an exposure of abnormal proportions. It was ill-advised of the British government to procure the banning of the television programme, *Real Lives—At the Edge of the Union*, starring Northern Ireland extremists, in July 1985. Aside from the publicity generated, and the upturn in contributions received by the American fund Noraid, some real damage must have been caused to the BBC External Services. Even so, there was something bogus about the insistence, largely on the part of people working in television, that it was 'downright insulting to the British public not to let them see and judge for themselves'. A lot of what is televised is, one would suppose, an insult to the British public, and the fact that rubbish or worse continues apace doesn't say much for that public's ability to judge for themselves—or else for the effectiveness of the protests of those who do protest. Strong words such as 'insult' and 'honour' and 'dignity' provoke one to look carefully at their users.

118

Underneath such commotions lurks the ancient fear of intellectuals that an individual banning will lead to wholesale proscription, that if *Sweets of Sin* is given to the flames so will *Ulysses* be. This implies meagre faith in *anybody's* judgement. The general public, in the limited form in which I meet it, although urged by a more particular public to 'join the debate', had little to say about the *Real Lives* affair. But letters in the *Radio Times* welcomed the ensuing journalists' strike (itself no doubt connected with honour) for relieving them for twenty-four hours of the customary unending round of horrors and making room for something they enjoyed, such as music. Withholding one's labour is a risky measure.

*

Well-meant attempts at de-censorship or rehabilitation can be risky too, as witness the 1963 conference in Czechoslovakia on the question of Kafka, in which Marxist speakers concluded that, for all his pessimism, Kafka was a progressive humanist writer and hence properly part of the true Communist tradition. Some contended that he was pre-eminent in revealing the alienation of man under capitalism; it was bourgeois capitalist critics who had smothered him under metaphysical metaphors and mysteries. Günter Grass has observed that several of the participants in the conference were subsequently expelled from the Communist party or—in the case of its chairman—fled their country.

A young Malaysian poet was officially reprimanded for alluding to his home town as 'Sleepy Hollow'; not a bad description of that pleasant little place, Malacca—but such is the susceptibility of new nations. (One of Jean Giraudoux's characters opined that the finest thing nationhood ever did by gathering scattered individuals into one body was to replace duelling by war.) The poet has since published a number of poems to the effect that when he ought to have been explicit he was poetical, that he has been too detached (or possibly afraid) and the time has come to make up for the years of silence. These purely abstract declarations of future intent proved sufficient by themselves, and he has since thought fit to emigrate.

119

When banning is impossible because the object is too deeply rooted in people's consciousness, some other device must be sought. The Nazis couldn't condone Heine's Jewishness, but neither could they consign his so Germanic poem on the Lorelei to oblivion. So in their song-books they attributed it to 'author unknown'. It had become a genuine folk-ballad.

Not all cases are as half-way happy as 'The Fate of Epigrams', recorded by a Czech poet, Jaromír Hořec, in 1957. First the epigram in question couldn't be published because it attacked someone in a high position; then it couldn't be published because it lacked topicality, the subject having been removed from office. We wonder how much has been so successfully banned or hushed up that no one has heard tell of it. Executions don't always give the executed a new lease of life. Once again the ironic perspective fails to allay our fears.

*

Ironies relating to the concentration camps—'even a black market is better than none at all'—must be rare, and are best left to those who experienced them at first hand. Karl Kraus's reflections on the subject are allowable because he was writing early in the proceedings (1933), about what seemed merely a new development in state security in neighbouring Germany. He quotes from newspaper reports of prisoners getting depressed and dying primarily, the doctors say, because they have lost the will to live, and of others who misbehaved to the extent of inflicting wounds on themselves while *en route* to the camp, or else—such was the deplorable state of their health to begin with—fainted near open windows and fell to their death in the yard below. Kraus explains that obviously those who have undergone what is called an 'educational cure' in the hope of 'a spiritual rehabilitation' cannot themselves testify to the success of their treatment 'because the spiritual transformation which often occurs at a stroke not infrequently results in unconsciousness or at least an impaired memory, and because astonishment at unaccustomed things may result in speech disorders'.

120

Trade Ironies

ONE evening Alfred de Musset is sitting in an almost empty theatre. The play is by Molière, an old bungler who knew nothing of the fine art of tickling the fancy and serving up an exquisitely cooked denouement. Thank God, authors have improved their techniques since then!

So much for irony at the expense of the philistines and the trendies . . . Observing how common sense had inspired genius, Musset marvels at Molière's passion for the harsh truth, his profound knowledge of the world. One laughs when one ought to be weeping. But is it enough to admire, then depart without taking due note?

He notices a lovely girl whose delicate neck brings to mind an undistinguished verse by Chénier. (That won't offend Molière's shade, will it?) Musset would gladly emulate Molière if he could, and take up satire's whip. But when the play ends he finds himself following the girl to her door. His soul has willed one thing, his body another. What remains in his head is Chénier's image of a white, delicate neck.

The poem in which Musset tells this chastening story is entitled 'A Wasted Evening'. (Well, the girl was accompanied by her mother.)

*

Books you were going to write with letters for titles. Have you read his F? O yes, but I prefer Q. Yes, but W is wonderful. O yes, W. Remember your epiphanies on green oval leaves, deeply deep, copies to be sent if you died to all the great libraries of the world, including Alexandria? Someone was to read them there after a few thousand years . . . When one reads

121

these strange pages of one long gone one feels that one is at one with one who once . . .

Given the delights that irony holds out for writers, it is not surprising that, despite the strictures writers have brought against irony, the subject of writing and reading should have received special ironic treatment. Pegasus has frequently been stung by shafts feathered from his own wings.

'Nowadays,' Goethe is reported as having said in 1806, 'books are not written to be read, to impart information and instruction; they are written to be reviewed.' A hundred years on, and what progress has been made? A character in Edith Wharton's story, 'Expiation', innocently supposes that every book has to stand or fall on its own merits. 'Bosh!' her friend tells her:

That view is as extinct as the post-chaise and the packet-ship—it belongs to the time when people read books. Nobody does that now; the reviewer was the first to set the example, and the public were only too thankful to follow it. At first they read the reviews; now they read only the publishers' extracts from them. Even these are rapidly being replaced by paragraphs borrowed from the vocabulary of commerce.

Since publishers have quite legitimately come into the picture—rather obscurely, Schlegel wrote that publishing was to thinking as the maternity ward was to the first kiss—we move forward thirty years to the publisher's advertisement, a self-inflicted irony, reproduced in *Culture and Environment*:

A BOOK FOR THE FEW
120th thousand,

and then another fifty years, to hear the publisher Robert Giroux telling us, in 1981, that 'acquiring editors used to be known by their authors; now some of them are known by their restaurants'. More recently (1985) a publisher's advertisement for a paperback quoted from a review of the hardback edition in *Mail on Sunday*: 'If a nastier, more vicious or distasteful novel appears this spring, I shall be surprised. But there is unlikely to be a better one either.'

This is simply an updated version of 'A BOOK FOR THE FEW . . .'

*

Evelyn Waugh observed of his father that 'He genuinely liked books—quite a rare taste today', while it is said of a character in *Catch-22* that 'He knew everything about literature except how to enjoy it.' Ah well, that could be said of many of us; as George Eliot's Dorothea lamented, it does seem as if people get worn out on the way to great thoughts, 'and can never enjoy them because they are too tired'. 'Give me a drink,' cried D. H. Lawrence, exasperated by Melville's sententiousness, 'that's what I want just now.' In Nigel Williams's *Star Turn* (1985) mention is made of writers who 'efface themselves in order to shine', who are dying to see reviews of their books in all the newspapers 'with words like UNOBTRUSIVELY BRILLIANT written over them in letters eight feet high'. (Who can they be? They sound rather nice guys, as writers go.) While in Böll's splendid story, 'Murke's Collected Silences', a young talks editor in the cultural department, sick to death of the pretentious guff he deals with (in two talks by a best-selling spiritual thinker the word 'art' occurred 134 times), cuts out the bits of tape where the speaker has paused for a rare moment, splices them together, and for the sake of his sanity plays the tape back at home in the evenings.*

The ironies spring out in all directions. We gather that as the mentally sick recover, so the art they produce deteriorates in originality and power. It is as well to keep in mind Robert Musil's counter-irony: 'The fact is that for some reason or other the notion that things of the mind never can have any real success whatsoever is more appealing than the notion of some colleague or other being successful with the products of *his* mind.' He could have been thinking of Milosz's too quick despairers, or of those

---

*In a supporting irony, the offices of the broadcasting company boast ashtrays of beaten copper, so handsome—they had won a design award—and so expensive that no one dares soil them, and the floor around is littered with cigarette ends and ash. Not unlike a British pub.

gentlemen, described by George Eliot, who 'have made an amazing figure in literature by general discontent with the universe as a trap of dullness into which their great souls have fallen by mistake'.

*

Poets are favourite targets, possibly because writers who don't write it (and also some who do) consider poetry either a soft option or inclined to put on airs, and its practitioners at one only in their vanity. Nietzsche observed that poets crave an audience, even if only of buffaloes; and in 'How to Tell a Major Poet', E. B. White came up with the answer: anyone who, when reading from his or her own works, experiences a choked feeling. Orwell considered that one had the right to expect ordinary decency 'even of a poet'; and a character in Kipling's 'The Horse Marines', having quoted a passage from Macaulay's 'The Armada', draws the company's attention to the fact that it is true as well as beautiful: 'That's rare in poetry, I'm told.'* And Brecht declared that those who write against rain and those who are opposed to the phases of the moon, if they have a nice turn of phrase, can achieve fame. She too, said Marianne Moore in a poem, disliked it, 'all this fiddle', which (Auden) 'makes nothing happen'. It was Macaulay, not necessarily taking the tip from the mentally ill, who reckoned that 'as civilization advanced, poetry must almost inevitably decline. Alex Comfort (fouling his own love-nest, one might think) has opined that

*There is a (surely apocryphal) story to the effect that, challenged with the couplet

> I, John Sylvester,
> Lay with your sister,

Jonson countered with

> I, Ben Jonson,
> Lay with your wife.

When the other man objected that this was not a rhyme, Jonson retorted: 'No, but it is *true*.' More commonly rhyme comes out on top. Boileau complained that when he wanted to summon up a writer *sans défaut*, reason said Virgil, but rhyme dictated a third-rater by the name of *Quinault*.

With better things in hand
no one would dip a pen,

while Huck Finn's book, *Friendship's Offering*, was 'full of beautiful stuff and poetry; but I didn't read the poetry'.

*

Mere mischievousness, one might reckon, the servants of the Muse nervously mocking their promiscuous mistress, and not to be taken too seriously. But Tonio Kröger is in dead earnest when he tells Lisabeta Ivanovna, a friend to whom he confides all his troubles:

I may be standing upon some platform, in some hall in front of people who have come to listen to me. And I find myself looking round among my hearers, I catch myself secretly peering about the auditorium, and all the while I am thinking who it is that has come here to listen to me, whose grateful applause is in my ears . . . I do not find what I seek, Lisabeta, I find . . . the same old gathering of early Christians, so to speak: people with fine souls in uncouth bodies, people who are always falling down in the dance, if you know what I mean; the kind to whom poetry serves as a sort of mild revenge on life. Always and only the poor and suffering, never any of the others, the blue-eyed ones, Lisabeta—they do not need mind . . .

And, after all,. would it not be a lamentable lack of logic to want it otherwise? . . . The kingdom of art increases and that of health and innocence declines on this earth. What there is left of it ought to be carefully preserved; one ought not to tempt people to read poetry who would much rather read books about the instantaneous photography of horses.*

Thoughts not utterly dissimilar must have passed through the minds of at least some poets as they stood at the lectern. Do they really want to read to the sort of people who want to be read to by people like them? Better an audience of buffaloes.

*Or geniuses taking snaps of geniuses, Musil would have groaned. 'What this age demonstrates when it talks of the genius of a racehorse or a tennis-player is probably less its conception of genius than its mistrust of the whole higher sphere of things' (*The Man Without Qualities*).

Lisabeta, herself a painter, has an answer ready, a short one. The solution to the problem that is upsetting him, she says, is that he is 'quite simply, a bourgeois . . . a bourgeois on the wrong path, a bourgeois *manqué*'. 'Thank you, Lisabeta,' he says: 'now I can go home in peace. I am expressed.'

*

Karl Kraus's yearnings were akin to Tonio Kröger's: to be at one with real life, with the blue-eyed ones, 'to sit just once more at a fully occupied table; to hear once more the belches of *joie de vivre*; to squeeze the sweaty hand of love-thy-neighbour'. And some good fairy has made his wish come true. 'I'm in the thick of it, the earth has me again—for someone has stolen my fur coat!' People are interested in him, they pity him, they admire him, they forgive him.

As Voltaire noted, our instinct is to pursue what flies from us and to fly from what pursues us. People stop Kraus in the street to condole with him; all this solidarity is unbearable; next the income-tax collectors will descend on him. 'I wrote books, but people understood only the coat.' He locks himself inside his house. But he has one hope left. 'By publishing a new book I might manage to make the Viennese forget me.'

Yet the most poignant of these professional *cris de cœur* sounds when Proust is describing the maids, Céleste and Marie. 'They will never read any books, but neither will they ever write any.' This must be the only kind word a writer has ever found to say for non-readers.

*

Irony, as opposed to plain dissent, is rarely encountered in serious-minded television programmes, though it may be inspired in the minds of viewers. In popular programmes we find plenty of what is more accurately termed sarky banter. In *Coronation Street* (6 March 1985) a pompous know-all advises a young fellow never to give his address to a girl he takes out, and never to take out a girl who lives near him. 'Oh?' says the young fellow. 'Is that why you never take your missus out?' Such incidental jokiness can afford comfort through the deflation or defusing it effects. In the same instalment of the same series a woman is the subject of a humiliating story in the local newspaper. A friend consoles her: 'Today's sensation is tomorrow's wrapping round fish and chips.'

Television is not loath to make fun of its own great thoughts on occasion, generally in a bland fashion, though sometimes quite pointedly. In a comedy series two young girls are forbidden to go to a rock concert. One of them says, 'Our parents think something will happen to us.' 'Yes,' says the other: 'I blame television—those programmes, all silhouettes and social workers.' That television can be ironic about itself, however innocuously, sustains our faith in its future. Which one trusts will be rather smaller than its present.

Love and Death

THE great real-life irony, of course, concerns death. This 'sensible warm motion', which we have known as long and as intimately as we have known anything, becomes 'a kneaded clod'. Perhaps something better, or something worse, happens to the spirit, the 'delighted spirit' Claudio called it, capable of delight and therefore of the opposite. We can't be sure of that, but certainly something radical happens. The death of oneself is hard to believe, yet there are no two ways about the kneaded clod; that we have seen with our own eyes.

Something so alive can become so lifeless. 'Huddl'd in dirt the reasoning engine lies,' as Rochester harshly puts it, 'Who was so proud, so witty and so wise.' Even those notoriously avid for posterity's favour, and most confident of it, draw back when they remember the price of admission:

> If I can't be famous till I'm dead
> I'm in no great hurry to be read.

We may, or some of us may, console ourselves with the thought that we shall rest in peace—but when did we want peace, except in the smallest of remedial doses? A whole eternity of it?

The alternative to dying is living for ever, in the same old way. But this is an ambition that has provoked many ironies in the line of 'he that findeth his life shall lose it'. A model for the more vulgar class of them is provided by the man who underwent treatment for rejuvenation and was found dead in bed the morning before he was due to give a lecture on 'How I was made twenty years younger by Eugen Steinach'. How much finer are the courageous ironies of the Duchess of Malfi: who would be afraid of death,

> Knowing to meet such excellent company
> In th'other world?

Asked if the strangler's cord doesn't strike terror, she replies,

> Not a whit:
> What would it pleasure me to have my throat cut
> With diamonds? or to be smothered
> With cassia? or to be shot to death with pearls?

*

And of course the runner-up must be love, that most precious and powerful of emotions, the most altruistic and the most selfish, both bane and boon, to lack which is woe, to own which is wound, 'the bright foreigner, the foreign self', inspiring an unprecedented delicacy, expressing itself in ludicrous or undignified ways, and itself subject—so the evidence indicates—

to sudden death or slow dereliction, often accompanied by the pettiest of feelings and the most ignoble of machinations.

To start with, either the unnerving if intriguing procedures of successful courtship—Prospero, a careful father, knew that light winning makes the prize light—or else the pains of unrequited affection, so absurd in the eyes of the unengaged beholder. Dick Swiveller never nursed a dear Gazelle but when it came to know him well it was sure to marry a market-gardener. 'I have seen some of the best women merely passing the time of day with an intelligent man (not myself, by the way),' Stendhal writes in his taxonomy, *De l'amour*, 'while at the same time, and indeed almost in the same breath, they were lost in the admiration of utter fools.' Or, as Yeats has it,

> It's certain that fine women eat
> A crazy salad with their meat.

But 'this is the monstruosity in love, lady, that the will is infinite, and the execution confined; that the desire is boundless, and the act a slave to limit'. I take this classic passage as not to be understood solely in a physical, comical-coarse sense. Nor in that of the story about the man in bed with his girl-friend during an air raid, who pleads, 'Perfect fear casteth out love.'

Perfect love, too, can cast out love. The narrator of Goethe's poem, 'The Diary', whose coach has broken down, picks up a pretty girl, a virgin at that, at the inn, but his usual healthy appetite lets him down. It is love for the woman he is on his way home to that has inhibited him. With nothing better in hand, he dips his pen and writes some 'secret words' in his journal: *'Illness is the truest test of health.'** Stendhal holds out hope on the subject of what he calls *fiasco*; the knowledge that it is a very common misfortune should decrease the risk of its occurrence.

Then there is the little difference between the sexes. 'Most men seek a proof of love which they consider dispels all doubt; women

---

*T. J. Reed sums up rather more wittily (*Goethe*, 1984): 'Such is the potency of a natural morality—or the morality of a natural impotence.'

are not lucky enough to be able to find a like proof,' Stendhal writes. 'It is one of life's misfortunes that what brings certainty and happiness to one lover brings danger and almost humiliation to the other.' I think he means that whereas the proof of a woman's love is that she yields to the man, an unambiguous physical action situated in the present, the proof of a man's love is solely a moral matter and lies in the future. Whether what he says still holds good is a question I would not wish to pronounce on; and likewise his opinion that 'a long siege humiliates a man, but ennobles a woman'. But Matthew Prior's verse 'A True Maid', though undeniably a period piece of male chauvinism, is impossible to resist:

> No, no; for my virginity,
>> When I lose that, says Rose, I'll die:
> Behind the elms, last night, cried Dick,
>> Rose, were you not extremely sick?

Men have died and the worms have eaten them, but not for love—that is one brisk and bracing and fallacious view; many, we know, have killed for love, and some, we can be pretty sure, have died because of it. In the delirium of love and death during carnival time in the sanatorium on the magic mountain, Hans Castorp plays on the similarity in sound between *l'amour* and *la mort*: 'They are both of them carnal, love and death, and hence their terror and their great magic!'

It was always carnival time with Nero. In Racine's *Britannicus* (1669) when Junie is hustled in, conveniently clad in her night attire, he is turned to stone by the sight of her, unadorned, silent, and defenceless, in striking contrast to the fierce soldiers and the torches and the noise surrounding her. He is as near to being in love as he can be. Julien Sorel, in *Le Rouge et le Noir* (1830), is a cooler customer than either Castorp or Nero, or so it would seem. Animated by class resentment, he plans the seduction of the pure and loving Mme de Rênal like a military operation, timing every move. Not surprisingly, he doesn't much enjoy the actual event, but a few days later he finds he is madly in love with the lady. Not that the story has a happy ending, for the deserving young man on the make loses his head. 'Never had that head been so poetic as at the moment when it was about to fall'; we read of Julien's execution that 'It all passed simply, respectably, and on his part without affectation.'

Can we bear further Proustian ironies, this time from his first book, *Les Plaisirs et les jours*, published when he was twenty-five? He knew, he says in one of the sketches, a little boy of ten, precocious in imagination, who had conceived an intellectual passion for a slightly older girl. He would stand in front of his window to see her pass, weeping if he didn't see her, weeping even more bitterly if he did. One day he threw himself out of the window. Why? There were various theories—that he was in despair at not seeing her: but he had just had a long conversation with her, and she had been unusually kind; that he felt he could never again expect such great pleasure, and the rest of his life would be insipid. The truth, he had confided to a friend, was that he always felt keenly disappointed when he saw her, but once she was absent his imagination restored her to her former power of fascination and he yearned to see her again. There was only one way of escaping from this circle of pain.

Proust adds that the boy lived for many years afterwards, a hopeless idiot, having escaped into utter forgetfulness. The girl insisted on marrying him, against all advice, but he never recognized her.

The mystery at the heart of love, to outsiders a source of bewilderment or ironic amusement, is illustrated by the story, in the same volume, of Mme de Breyves, who is in love with the absent M. de Laléande, once glimpsed at a soirée. If what she loved in him was his good looks, then her friends could hope to find a more handsome young man to distract her. If she loved his intelligence, they might put someone more intelligent in her way. But he is neither handsome nor intelligent. Nor is there any evidence that he is faithful (or fickle), tender (or brutal), generous (or mean). It must be *him* she loves, or her conception of him, and there is no replacing that; since her sickness has no reason, it can have no remedy. M. de Laléande, virtually invisible, undistinguished to the point of inexistence, would be astonished to learn how 'he' is leading a miraculously heightened, abundant, sustained, and all-subduing existence in someone else's soul.

When love and death collide, we have either the irony of love destroyed or the irony of death defeated. In death's defeat— 'Many waters cannot quench love, neither can the floods drown it'—there is that true paradise, though 'lost', in a less mundane sense than Proust intended. When love is defeated, there are the Jacobean set pieces, the best and most complex occurring in Tourneur's *The Revenger's Tragedy*:

> Thou sallow picture of my poison'd love,
> My study's ornament, thou shell of death,
> Once the bright face of my betrothed Lady . . .
> And now methinks I could e'en chide myself
> For doting on her beauty . . .
> Does the silkworm expend her yellow labours
> For thee? For thee does she undo herself?
> Are lordships sold to maintain ladyships
> For the poor benefit of a bewitching minute?*

And so on, as Vindice's passionate outburst over the skull of his mistress degenerates into cynical reflections on highwaymen risking their lives to keep drabs in comfort and on erstwhile offers of twenty pounds per night (presumably for the sake of a few bewitching minutes of it).

*

Less elevated is the subject of love charms and aphrodisiacs, which, as old Chinese novels warn us when at last they get round

---

*Cf. the old ironies of war, and Wilfred Owen's poem, 'Futility', about the young soldier lying dead in the sun:

> Was it for this the clay grew tall?
> —O what made fatuous sunbeams toil
> To break earth's sleep at all?

to the moral, give with one hand and take away with the other.* As soon as he has the promised elixir, Sir Epicure Mammon will make an old man of fourscore a child. 'No doubt. He's that already,' his sceptical friend interjects. It has been pointed out that the Latin *venenum* meant both love-potion and poison. But I doubt that any irony was ever intended, since (*a*) love-philtres not infrequently did poison the recipients, and (*b*) the word also signified that which, whether for better or for worse, possessed the power to alter the natural quality of something else.

Yet a contingent irony may be in order. There is a medieval story about a young man who boasted at a convivial gathering that he possessed a cake which would cause any women who ate it to fall in love with him. A bold or sceptical girl took up the challenge, and he gave her a piece of ordinary cake that he happened to have on him. Later the girl wondered whether what she had swallowed could truly be the Devil's bread and, unable to sleep, she went to the young man's room to have it out with him. She remained there for the rest of the night. The priest who recounted this tale praised the excellence of the young man in that he had refrained from invoking the illicit help of the Devil.

We still live in the tag-end of Mr Mercaptan's era—he who preached brilliantly on 'that melancholy sexual perversion known as continence'—and hence Professor Heller can be forgiven for showing some surprise on hearing that a good half of his East Coast university class was undergoing psychoanalytical treatment for 'repressed chastity'. Be sure your virtue will find you out.

*

Allan Rodway has said, apropos of the 'dispassionate

---

*In this respect functioning like smutty talk. In his 'Essay on Poetry' (1682) John Sheffield, Duke of Buckinghamshire, complained of Rochester's verse that

> . . . obscene words, too gross to move desire,
> Like heaps of fuel, only choke the fire.

Poets oughtn't to go around choking the fires of passion—

> On other themes, he well deserves our praise,
> But palls that appetite he meant to raise.

133

objectivity' involved, that the ironist 'seems to give light rather than heat, since he has maturity enough to see round a question and not to be blinded by wrath'. True, wrath is as deleterious to irony as an attack of hiccups. But—light? It will not always be the kind that goes with sweetness. And Muecke writes that the ironist 'cannot help feeling as a man, but irony itself is a matter of seeing not feeling: it is based on intellect not sentiment'. The divorce between intellect and sentiment is one of whose genuineness I have never been convinced. These assertions suggest that the ironist, *au-dessus de la mêlée*, operates *de haut en bas*. Even the champions of irony can fail to appreciate sufficiently the feeling in it: the feeling—of fellow-suffering, of indignation, of horror, of pity—that accompanies the seeing. The intellect is more easily stopped in its tracks, and switched off, than is the heart. And sentiment—to preserve Muecke's terminology—will draw on, will press into service, a not always willing intellect.

When Macduff learns of the killing of his family, he is incredulous, 'in shock' as we say today. His wife? His children too? All of them? Not so much incredulity as the remote hope of some small remission. 'Dispute it like a man,' Malcolm tells him. (Like Macbeth, Malcolm has no children.) And he replies, in one of Shakespeare's most heart-rending passages,

> I shall do so;
> But I must also feel it as a man.
> I cannot but remember such things were
> That were most precious to me.

Then he recovers himself; that's to say, he returns to his role as a soldier, to the 'manly tune' of revenge, as dictated by reason, his grief (as Malcolm has urged) converted to expedient anger, his heart not blunted but sharpened by rage.

The clash between what is believed in general and what is felt on specific occasions is plain in Kobayashi Issa's haiku, written shortly after the death of his only child, towards the end of the eighteenth century:

> The world of dew is
> A world of dew, yet even
> So, yet even so . . .

As a Buddhist, Issa knew that this world and all in it is transitory, that all flesh is—not even grass—the dew on the grass, that death is commonplace and not to be railed against. Why, Jonson asked in similar circumstances, should man lament the state he ought to envy? But all the same . . . We should think the less of Issa, and of Jonson and Macduff, if for a while at least the intellect did not yield to feeling, and theory to actuality. They are themselves aware of the contradiction, between the Buddhist and the father, the warrior and the family man, the pessimist and the parent; their intelligence is not in question.

The irony here is faint; perhaps I am mistaken in supposing there to be any. Either way, ironies relating to death, the death of children in particular, don't afford much comfort. But then, what does?

Sarcasm, the Mighty Brought Low, the Last Laugh

IN his *Memoirs of a Malayan Official* (1965) Victor Purcell remarked, a trifle hyperbolically, that he ruined his career in the Malayan Civil Service at the outset, in 1921, by opting to enter the branch known as the Chinese Protectorate. Its function was widely regarded, he said, as being 'not so much to protect the Chinese as to protect the country *against* them', they being so

135

smart and diligent. In reviewing the book I commented, with would-be irony, that if it were granted that a colonial official could ever do good, then Purcell had done good in protecting Chinese women against various forms of exploitation. This drew a savage letter from a reader, attacking me for sneering fashionably at colonial officers, one of whom he had himself been. I replied in mollifying manner, but heard no more. I had offended him by my unrecognized irony; I had offended him afresh, and perhaps more grievously, by pointing out the irony. All he had seen was routine sarcasm.

*

In August 1984 *The Times* reported that a dozen or so people were said to have committed suicide in Bucharest because their dwellings were about to be demolished to make room for a new civic palace of culture. This is an instance of irony of an indeterminate, shifting kind.* An action designed to enhance the quality of life has resulted in misery and death. Yes, but our reaction is likely to be modified by the suspicion that civic palaces of culture do not invariably have very much to do with the quality of life. The ironic effect is immediate, but it fades on consideration. (Our smiles do not fade since they never materialized.)

The very word 'culture' is devious, inviting to so many ironies that one hardly dare use it except in connection with pearls and biologists. (The great majority of the world's population never have used it, although they are fairly conversant with 'book', 'music', 'painting', so the expression 'minority culture' is probably pleonastic.) 'Culture' may suggest preciosity, 'anxious for to shine in the high aesthetic line', or a shelf of handsomely bound and unbroached copies of Great Books of the World or dusty busts of Caesar and Beethoven; or it may relate to the ways

---

*Also, I fear, of what Schlegel terms 'coarse irony', as 'found in the real nature of things' and 'properly at home in the history of mankind'. Less coarse, even so, than what elsewhere he adduced as some people's idea of irony—knowing how many children Laura had. And certainly less vulgar than Byron:

> Think you, if Laura had been Petrarch's wife,
> He would have written sonnets all his life?

in which primitive tribes prepare their food, bury their dead or eat them, or circumcise their young females. It can mean being exhorted to read books, listen to music, etc. favoured by a particular government, and being prevented from reading books, listening to music, etc. disapproved by a particular government. It might be felt that in some of its appearances, for example 'Ministry of Culture', 'Cultural Revolution', even 'Cultural Attaché', the word signifies the opposite of what it has often been thought to mean. ('Culture Shock' is jet-set hyperbole; I recall some British visitors in Japan telling me they could never live in a place where they couldn't read the London Sunday papers, hot from the press, in bed.) It is a pity that Hanns Johst—not, as it happened, Goering—got in first with the remark about reaching for his Browning (not the poet) whenever he heard the word 'culture'. Rather than one's pistol, one should reach for one's suitcase, and a ticket out of the country.

The irony basic to *The Man Without Qualities*, a work that Muecke, in mildly taxonomic mood, calls 'as complete a textbook for General Irony as Swift is for Impersonal Irony and Thomas Mann for Romantic Irony', is that the novel centres on the preparations, largely cultural in nature, being made in 1913 to mark the seventieth anniversary, in 1918, of the accession to the Austrian throne of Franz Josef, 'Emperor of Peace'. Writing in the 1920s, Musil knew that the celebrations would never take place, and not only because Franz Josef died in 1916. Through his hero Ulrich, and specifically by way of an essay on Love of Country that Ulrich wrote at school (and was almost expelled for), Musil invokes the very highest authority in support of his ironies: 'even God probably preferred to speak of His world in the subjunctive of potentiality . . . for God makes the world and while doing so thinks that it could just as easily be some other way.'*

Possibly it is only one's distrust of institutionalism that deters

---

*H. L. Mencken carries the thought further when asking, in one of his contributions to theology, why we should assume that the God who presumably created the universe is still running it. 'It is certainly perfectly conceivable that He may have finished it and then turned it over to lesser gods to operate.'

one from smiling wholeheartedly over the Institute for Popular-
ization of Humour of Nations. Sited in Gabrovo, Bulgaria, the
Institute maintains a cultural centre known as the House of
Humour and Satire, whose unifying motto, we are told in a hand-
out, is 'The World Lasts Because It Laughs' (*sic*). There is a hint
of coercion here, the distant sound of dutiful jollity, a suggestion
of tightness behind the grin. Still, one would like the world to last
if possible. And in 1985 the Deputy Culture Minister of East
Germany complained that 'the lightness of life is not being taken
seriously enough' by the country's film industry. The heroes of
comedies, he urged, should be seen doing their social duty but 'in
an attractive and amusing way, and thus ultimately confirm the
optimism of our socialist life'. So much for humour. As for its
more subversive (or more ethical) relative, Kraus's saying comes
to mind: 'Satires which the censor understands are rightly
prohibited.'

And that saying recalls one of Brecht's. When in 1935/6 Sidney
Hook protested against Stalin's persecution of innocent people,
Brecht is alleged to have replied: 'The more innocent they are, the
more they deserve to die.' The extenuations commentators have
advanced for this shocking epigram are that Brecht was snapping
back in an ill-considered fashion or else he was being deliberately
provocative. But it has also been suggested that he was implying
something rather different: that those who were innocent of plot-
ting against Stalin deserved to die precisely for that reason.
Which would be a callous irony, but at least witty—and more generally acceptable. It is unlikely that we shall ever know whether
Brecht was being satirical or maladroitly nasty; though we may
have our suspicions.

*

In connection with the 'intro trouble' that afflicts journalists,
their need not merely for a compelling first sentence but for a
compelling first word, Philip Howard has listed just a few of the
'meanings' for which the word 'Ironically' has been used. Thus:

1. By a tragic coincidence
2. By an exceptional coincidence
3. By a curious coincidence
4. By a coincidence of no importance
5. You and I know, of course, though other less intelligent mortals walk benighted under the midday sun
6. Oddly enough, or it's a rum thing that
7. Oh hell! I have run out of words for starting a sentence with.

And Nicholas Bagnall sums up with the comment that for writers in a hurry there are only two kinds of irony: 'one makes you laugh, the other cry. If you laugh it's gentle, if you cry it's bitter.' An instance of slackly *soi-disant* irony, located towards the bitter end of this meagre spectrum, came in a television news report in June 1985, at the height of the hijacking of a TWA plane, about a man with a rifle breaking into the State Department in Washington and shooting a woman. Presumably the incident was termed ironic because it exposed a weakness in security at the very headquarters of security, near the office of the Secretary of State. In the event it turned out to be not a terrorist action but a domestic quarrel: the man had killed his mother and then himself. *There* was the true though unremarked irony—killing the one who gave you birth.

In J. G. Ballard's novel, *Empire of the Sun* (1984), the British doctor in the Japanese prison camp points out an irony which could make you laugh and cry simultaneously. When the stock of cigarettes runs out, condoms become the main unit of currency, and the number in circulation remains practically constant during the three years that follow. The doctor reflects that the value of the condom actually rises despite the impotence or sterility of the enfeebled inmates. But the secret wisdom discovered by Goethe's traveller—that illness was the truest test of health—would find no place there.

There is a special satisfaction in seeing the mighty brought low, all the greater if brought low by the humble or feeble. Or by a midget. Frank Gonzalez-Crussi, a pathologist, tells of a giant American Indian who fought his way all round the world as a seaman, took shotgun pellets by the bucketful without noticing them, and was too huge for the autopsy table to accommodate his body. It was, the pathologist says none too aptly, by 'no small irony' that he came to the table: he had succumbed to a tapeworm scarcely three millimetres long.

Comparable is the fate of the Martian invaders in *The War of the Worlds*; nothing could save humanity from this all-powerful enemy except those 'microscopic allies', bacteria to which man is immune. (Less blessed are the knock-on effects of modern technology applied to agriculture, as accidentally foreseen in Ralph Hodgson's poem, 'Stupidity Street': no insects, so no birds, so no partridges to eat.) Elephants are terrified of mice. For want of a nail the rider was lost. A small trumpet caused the walls of Jericho to collapse; well, seven trumpets and some shouting. There has never yet been a philosopher who could endure the toothache patiently. Senator Buddenbrook died of a bad tooth, or of a bungled extraction by a dentist called—a case of proleptic irony?—Herr Brecht. And of course an all too rarely ironic poet has sung of Ozymandias, king of kings, reduced to two trunkless legs of stone and a shattered visage sinking into the desert sands, none of his works left, no one to look on them.

Fielding's Jonathan Wild laments the unhappy condition of the pickpocket who, while he is employing his hands in somebody else's pockets, cannot defend his own. And a related satisfaction, since we cannot leave justice solely to the official representatives of law and order, lies in seeing thieves fall out and betray one another, as happens in *Volpone*, or rogues exposing one another, as in the stories told by the Friar and the Summoner in the *Canterbury Tales*.

Chaucer's irony is normally too delicate, recessed in its context, as well as too charitable, to be extracted to much effect. We enjoy watching Chauntecleer, that elegant fowl so proud of his learning, bring himself down a peg:

> For, also siker as *In principio*,
> *Mulier est hominis confusio*;

> Madame, the sentence of this Latin is—
> Womman is mannes joye and al his blis.

Unless, that is, he is availing himself of the 'negative freedom' we shall note in Mr Bennet's dealings with his wife in *Pride and Prejudice*. Either way it remains true that Chauntecleer is smart, smarter than a fox, and saves his life by dint of natural, untutored intelligence, 'by kynde, and by noon other lore'.

*

Irony can fail through being too patently wrought, or because it is labour-intensive and gives off a smell of sweat. In Flaubert it seems at times a combination of both. Lilian R. Furst cites, as a 'pregnant' episode, as an unvoiced denigratory judgement on Charles Bovary (just look at his name: very subtle!), the account of the debauchery that leads to his failure in the medical examinations. He used to go to cafés and indulge in his passion for dominoes. Shutting himself every evening in a dirty public room and pushing around small sheepbones with black dots on them— for him this is an act of precious liberty, raising him in his self-esteem. It is an access to forbidden pleasures; when he enters the café, he places his hand on the doorknob 'with an almost sensual joy'. A real hero, a real man, a real medical student, would spend his evenings in a brothel with a bottle. We may feel that Flaubert placed his hand rather too heavily on the neck of his unfortunate character.*

When Bovary's horse stumbles as he enters Les Bertaux, the farm owned by Emma's father, 'the possibility of an ill omen immediately occurs to us,' Miss Furst remarks, 'though not to the unimaginative Charles'. It isn't hard for the reader to be cleverer than Charles. But what would we think of a suitor who turned back because his horse stumbled at the threshold of his loved one's home? Or rather, following the text, what would we think of a doctor who hesitated because his horse, frightened by dogs,

---

*'Even those of our novelists whose manner is most ironic pity life more and hate it less than M. de Maupassant and his great initiator Flaubert.' (Henry James, 'Guy de Maupassant', *Partial Portraits*.)

shied as he was on his way to treat an unknown farmer who happened to have a daughter? A stumbling or shying horse is no more than an unbrushed, ill-educated coincidence.

If Jane Austen could illustrate the evils of reading Gothic novels so lightly, why must Flaubert make heavy weather over the reading of trashy romances? And what do they matter, all these ironies, so long as Charles loves his wife? Ah, but that—that he does love his wife—is *the* irony, the big one.

*

In a paper entitled 'Theory and Teaching', Christopher Ricks cites a 'flexibly suggestive' formulation of Empson's, which in his view, and in mine, quite properly remains unerected into an elaborate theory. 'An irony has no point unless it is true, in some degree, in both senses; for it is imagined as part of an argument; what is said is made absurd, but it is what the opponent might say.'

Empson's principle, Ricks continues, serves to distinguish irony from 'its malignant sibling', sarcasm, which is 'inferior in its superiority'. It is the case that irony must be purged of any hint of conscious superiority: the question is one not of knowing better but of knowing otherwise; and the inferiority of sarcasm is indicated by its uncouth etymology, 'rending flesh'. Empson's principle also helps Ricks to understand the force of a poem called 'Streets'; which I shall quote in full since it seems not to be in print.

> The poem was entitled 'The Streets of Hanoi',
> It told of falling bombs and death and destruction
> And misery and pain and wastage.
> The poem was set to music, which told of death
> And destruction and misery and pain and wastage.
>
> A hall was found to play it in, a singer to sing it,
> An orchestra to accompany the singer, and a printer
> To print the programme . . . Whereupon it was felt
> (Things being what they happened to be) that
> The song had better be called 'The Streets of Saigon'.
>
> It was well sung, well played, and well received.

> Truly poetry is international, just like music,
> And falling bombs and death and destruction
> And misery and pain and wastage.
> Truly we only need one poet in the world
> Since local references can be inserted by editors,
> Theatre managers or clerks in the Culture Ministries.

The axis on which this poem turns, Ricks says, is the line, not to be misheard as sarcasm, 'Truly poetry is international, just like music'. He quotes Empson's words, 'true, in some degree, in both senses', adding: 'truly (and not just with sorrowful head-shaking at the preposterousness of such a thought) poetry *is* international, but not in the easy empty way which would suffocate political conscience—such as is true here and now—under the pseudo-transcendental verities (for Hanoi, read Saigon).'

The poem does, I see, accord with the principle—a common fate is always individual, and when a disaster strikes our street we don't think of it as an international phenomenon—yet it seems to me there is a heaviness about it, a labour-intensiveness manifested in its repetitions, and a trace of preachiness. The true ironist does not himself pass judgement, F. McD. C. Turner wrote, 'but appeals to our sense of truth and justice to do so'. If the ironist is seen to be passing judgement, pressing home a moral, then irony flies out of the window, if indeed it doesn't turn against the ironist himself. We may feel here that towards the end of the poem the author is having a go at a favourite target; his indignation isn't entirely disinterested, and his efforts to keep his cool (in other parts of the world Saigon will be changed to Hanoi) evince themselves in a stolid, too deliberate hypothermia.

His defence might be that what he describes in the first eleven lines is *true*; that it really did happen, as it happens. But we know that where art, including the art of irony, is concerned, this is no excuse. Since the author did not think fit to include the piece in his collected poems, we can suppose that he felt misgivings, possibly of a like nature.

*

143

Irony may be a last-ditch defence against—what humans cannot endure—meaninglessness, by identifying or postulating a connection or cross-reference and so registering or creating a sort of desperate almost-sense. V. S. Pritchett's definition, 'Satire is anger laughing at its own futility', applies equally well—or better—to irony. Which can have or be the last laugh. At times literally the last, as in St Laurence's famous words, when being slowly roasted on a gridiron: his executioners should turn him over, 'for this side is quite done'. In Umberto Eco's *The Name of the Rose* (1983) the grim monk Jorge of Burgos contends that the story proves how laughter is 'something very close to death and to the corruption of the body'. He condemns laughter for much the same reasons that have been advanced against irony: 'Laughing at evil means not preparing oneself to combat it, and laughing at good means denying the power through which good is self-propagating.'

Some accounts disclose that the torturers attempted to ward off Laurence's irony with one of their own, and with moderate success. They derided him for being too lazy to turn himself over. Hence the common expression, which I can't recall ever having come across myself, 'as lazy as Laurence'.

Chinese

WHEN I was making notes for this book I came, before long, to see irony everywhere. In the spirit of the quotation from *Tristram Shandy*, it assimilated everything to itself. Irony was the normal mode of apprehension and discourse; man's single state had long ago been shaken to bits, and nothing was but what was not. One might just as well set out to write a book about air or water or grass.

Then I broke off to visit China. Irony was mislaid at Heathrow; or else it had no valid passport. In the People's Republic either there was no irony at all, or it had changed into something unrecognizable; a rare twitch of the lips perhaps, or an averted eye. Naturally I enquired after it. There was air, there was water, there was grass. Oh yes, the Chinese said, there was a word which, according to the best dictionaries, translated into English as 'irony'. Examples, however, were not forthcoming. Possibly it was a politically sensitive topic. I had many years before grown used to occasional mysterious silences in the East; they seemed no worse, sometimes better, than the raucous noises which replace them in the West. As for the Chinese, it may be—given their history: 'most wrecked and longest of all histories'—that irony would have to be either total, and hence totally disabling, or else renounced *in toto*.

As it happened, at the time capitalism was ceasing to be a politically sensitive issue. That is, as a foreigner one could make acceptable little jokes about it, though otherwise it was now something to be thought about seriously and sincerely, preferably by someone else. I assured the Chinese that I was sincerely interested in irony, which to me seemed to possess, in certain circumstances, certain positive, constructive, and strengthening qualities. (The word 'certain' often appears in circumstances of uncertainty.) They listened seriously, and nodded their heads. There was a feeling in the air that conceivably something useful could be learned from foreigners, though it would need cautious sieving and supervising. Perhaps one touch of forgotten nature was about to make a comeback?

Eventually one among my captive audience, a friendly young man eager to learn and to teach, declared that he would write specifically for me a poem containing irony. Others promised to stay on the *qui vive*. I am still waiting. One can call spirits from the vasty deep—but will they come when one calls for them?

Irony was waiting for me, at Heathrow, when I returned. It seemed, I fancied, just a little chastened, less sure of itself. Or, more likely, I was.

*

Old Chinese ironies . . . Observing how wretchedly thin someone had grown, Li Po suggested that he must have been suffering from poetry again. And Po Chü-i, citing Lao-tzu's words: 'Those who speak know nothing; those who know are silent', asked how it was then that the man wrote an entire book. More feelingly, Su Tung-p'o mused on the birth of his son that usually parents wanted their child to be intelligent, yet he had wrecked his whole life through intelligence, and could only hope that the baby would prove ignorant and stupid—

> Then he will crown a tranquil life
> By becoming a Cabinet Minister.

That was a while ago, in the eleventh century, before the processes of government, as distinct from its personnel, had assumed their present proportions.

An embarrassment of a later period, a linguistic one, was recounted in a letter to *The Times* (20 July 1985) from a lady living in Coventry who, as a student physiotherapist, was required to help a Chinese patient out of bed and into a chair. The patient spoke no English, and her dictionary offered little practical guidance. Two of the phrases the hopeful young physiotherapist came upon were: 'I am sorry that your concubine is sick' and 'Here comes the Executioner'.

Of course the Chinese invented printing, and long ago. As they invented so many things. (There used to be a riddle: Why are we the wisest people in the world? For discovering the compass, and not discovering America.) More recently they have slipped back in technology, but sex—whatever the reticence surrounding it—is a different matter. There is illumination rather than irony in the report that people watching Roman Polanski's film *Tess* in Shandong Province were left cold by the love scenes but thrown into astonishment by the sight of a nineteenth-century threshing-machine far in advance of anything they were used to.

*

But, oh dear, a modern irony asserts itself, a sad one, divulged to us in hushed tones, though not as an example of irony, during that same visit. A bright young man, with a great future before him as an English interpreter, was sent to Hawaii to polish up his accent. Some local acquaintances gave him a couple of *Playboy* magazines, which he thought too amusing to throw away and so, when returning home, he packed them in his luggage, along with a motor-cyclist's helmet he had purchased. At Peking airport a metal sensor detected the helmet, the luggage was opened, and the magazines were revealed. Incitements to sex are unwelcome, and there were no pictures of agricultural machinery to offer in mitigation.

Disgrace ensued. The young man underwent several sessions of self-criticism in the presence of his 'work unit', was fined and also suspended from work for a time. The misdemeanour wouldn't have been fatal to his future; money had been invested in his training and English specialists were needed urgently. But such was the agony of it all that every scrap of the promising young man's English went clean out of his head. Shame had brainwashed him.

*

147

A brisk, assured young writer told us—rather bold of him, we thought—that he was descended from Confucius; he added that in this he was one among very many. Whatever guilt by association there may have been was thinly spread.

A memorial both ancient and modern, brought back from China, seems to raise not only the difficulty of conforming to authorized opinion in one's public utterances, when the party line can change so abruptly, but also the consequent uncertainty as to what one really thinks or feels in private, in the privacy of one's self. The mind, the sensibility, grow confused and then numb. This is indeed an Old Tale.

There were to be a thousand of them, Buddhas or something akin,
And every one of them different. He had finished 999,
And they were all and each, in some particular, different.
He had worked as fast as he could, but time was running out.

Now they came puffing up the hillside, abbots and priests,
Provincial governors and the usual lackeys; also (he feared)
An executioner from the Board of Punishments, severe of mien.
He strove to imagine the thousandth and its peculiar uniqueness.
They were just round the corner, the tally-man was shouting
'990 . . . 995 . . . 998 . . .' The executioner pursed his lips,
While the priests and the governors shaped the beginnings of a
Discreet smile. The Emperor was a stickler for punctuality.

The niche at least was ready. He jumped into it, cocking his head
And raising his hands in what he hoped was a brand-new position—
With luck they wouldn't notice that the thousandth was alive . . .
It wasn't. Some benign and witty divinity turned him into stone.
The sculptor was sculpture, the master his own masterpiece.

Much later came the new, the young, the red-blooded, licensed
To renounce the past and all its works. Ancient philosophers
Had been tried and condemned *in absentia*. Recent poets
Were sent to clean out latrines. The watchword was 'Realism!'
And now came the turn of the thousand Buddhas or whatever—
Equally unreal and irrelevant—they were. Crash, crash went
The sledge-hammers, demolishing the minute particulars and
Reducing uniquenesses. There was much to be done and undone.
They hastened to the thousandth. Crash went the hammers.

See, he has lost his head. But otherwise he is all there.
Which can hardly be said of some of us standing here,
Encouraged to gawk, now that policies have been slightly reversed
And the past is permitted. And we mutter ruefully an apt
And innocuous proverb: 'Easier to pull down than build up',
Cocking our heads, unsure what to do with our hands.

*

Incidentally, a friend who knows the Chinese language tells me that there was no indigenous word for humour, and hence a transliterated form was made up: 'yumo'. The characters chosen for the word, that is, to reproduce the sound—'yu' and 'mo'—mean respectively 'secluded' and 'silent'.

Negative Freedom

SO the ironist is negatively free; he is not bound by what he says, albeit he isn't exactly unbound by it. He may be virtuous, and yet indulge in cakes and ale, and then suffer from indigestion and crapulence. He frees himself from second-hand misery but without relieving those who experience it at first hand. He comes near to self-congratulation, not on simply avoiding some unhappy state of affairs but on simultaneously taking sad cognizance of it and neutralizing its effect on the bystander, himself. (We are reduced to the apophthegmatic form of expression, discredited

149

these days outside Zen circles, although once favoured by such as Kierkegaard, Schlegel, Goethe, Nietzsche, Kraus, etc.)

In this aspect irony, as its opponents have noted, becomes a means of depriving the object, whatever it is, of its reality in order that the subject, the ironist or the person to whom the irony is passed on, may feel free. It sounds like a feeble, self-protective transaction; still, sometimes a negative freedom, hurting nobody else, is all the freedom we can hope for, and if it helps us to carry on then it isn't to be sniffed at. When found drinking in the street as his theatre, the Drury Lane, burned down, Sheridan explained: 'A man may surely be allowed to take a glass of wine by his own fireside.' The humorous side of the good neighbour's broken leg didn't help the limb to mend any the faster, but it made her feel less lame. Stung in the course of peeling prawns, my wife was cheered by remembering that cogent anonymous couplet,

> *Cet animal est très méchant,*
> *Quand on l'attaque il se défend.*

And I can hope that my friend felt a little better when he wrote of his X-ray treatment, shortly before he died: 'Once a day — enough to make you sick!'

Known for his anarchist views, Herbert Read may have alleviated any embarrassment he felt at accepting a knighthood by explaining that he didn't feel important enough to refuse. Saul Bellow's famous thinker, Victor Wulpy, wasn't being self-depreciatory when he said of his fans, 'They want better clichés to live by'; he was complaining of persecution by his admirers and jeering at them (biting the hand etc.). But truly self-disparaging ironies are dangerous—'You wouldn't expect *me* to . . .' or 'I may not be Shakespeare . . .'—since they invite unironic agreement. In a combination of this mode and the Socratic, a friend of mine who wasn't getting on too well with the head of his university department posed after one little wrangle a rhetorical question expecting the answer No: 'I suppose you want me to resign?' The answer was Yes, and my friend, being something of a hero as well as an ironist, had no choice but to tender his resignation.

*

The habitual irony with which Mr Bennet in *Pride and Prejudice* treats his silly, obnoxious wife is compensation for his ineffectualness as a husband and a father. He has no compassion on her poor nerves, she complains. 'You mistake me, my dear. I have a high respect for your nerves. They are my old friends. I have heard you mention them with consideration these twenty years at least.' He makes no attempt to control her, or to protect his daughters from her damaging influence. He has given her up as incorrigible (was she corrigible once? He did marry her), and preserves his self-respect by means of urbane sarcasms which she is too stupid to notice, let alone take to heart. That's to say, he has made himself negatively free of his wife. It is a case of irony fallen back on by the defeated as a self-awarded consolation prize; at most it moves us to a pained smile.

One might surmise that Mr Bennet had turned ironic because he was henpecked. But ironists are more often born than made, even if there is plenty to make them. And in fact Kierkegaard asserted in his *Journals*—with that freedom from explanation and reservation that apophthegms allow—that a naturally ironic man will always be henpecked if he should marry.

While it would be foolhardy to confront fate without some form of armour, excessive reliance on what might be called the wrought-ironic—of which Mr Bennet's little speech about his wife's nerves is a specimen—provokes the question inspired by Andrew Young's crab:

> Does it make for death to be
> Oneself a living armoury?

*

Irony's armour helps us to bear the sufferings of others. Well, to succumb to them would help no one. A neglected writer commits

151

suicide in order to attract attention to his work; he at least is ready to die for the sake of fame. The work then draws unfavourable attention. We smile, because we cannot afford to shed tears for him; and he is well past being hurt by a smile, however snide. We would not inflict a show of our own quivering sensibility on a bereaved mother; but nor would we try to console her with clever remarks, even with irony's laconic wisdom. Face to face, we resort to harmless banalities which the sufferer understands in the spirit intended. This is a shared, almost you could say sacred, acknowledgement of inadequacy, and irony would never invade it.

Must Irony have a Victim? Can It be Sweet?

THAT irony is not necessarily a negation, a mortification visited on its victim or even a lessening of dignity, is demonstrated by a central incident in *Under Western Eyes*. Natalia Haldin, that pure idealistic soul, tells the narrator—an ignorant Englishman standing in for his author, a knowledgeable Pole—that 'this extraordinary man' Razumov is 'meditating some vast plan, some great undertaking; he is possessed by it—he suffers from it'. Actually Razumov is struggling to steer between the rock and the whirlpool: on one side the lawlessness of autocracy, on the other the lawlessness of revolution. His 'great undertaking' is to save his own life. He is no more than ordinary in wanting to make his way, unhelped by wealth or influence, within society as it is: which is hard enough without some rash young lover of freedom throwing himself on your mercy. That he suffers is true; and he suffers the more by falling in love, most unsuitably, with Natalia.

We think none the worse of Natalia for her grotesque error, grotesque in that it was Razumov who handed her beloved and heroic brother over to the Tsarist police. That she should think highly of him—with, as it turns out, some reason, though not the one in her mind—is further evidence of her goodness and generous nature. Perhaps a further irony, again causing her no damage in our eyes, lies in the fact that she and her kind are acceptable to neither party. The revolutionaries consider her aloof and passive, while the reactionaries are bound to distrust her fervid visions and philanthropic activities.

Dense as are the ironies of *Under Western Eyes*, they are simple compared with those which, from the title onwards, run through *Great Expectations*. Pip believes that Miss Havisham is his patron, as she is Estella's, and hence Estella is destined for him, he for her. But he is merely the 'brought-up London gentleman' owned by Magwitch: a convict's act of revenge upon society. Similarly, Estella has been brought up, her heart replaced by ice, to be the instrument of Miss Havisham's vengeance on men. Moreover, this supposedly genuine young lady is in fact Magwitch's daughter.

Given Pip's behaviour towards Joe Gargery and then towards his disastrous benefactor, it would seem wellnigh impossible to extricate him at all respectably from the weight of these ironies. To say the least, far more difficult than in the case of Natalia Haldin. And Dickens does not spare the young man. When Pip first hears of Herbert's Clara, he asks about her father: 'Living on—?' He has grown too interested in the financial nexus. The innocent, disinterested Herbert replies: 'On the first floor.'

But Pip is his own severest critic. (Apart from some modern ones: see Q. D. Leavis's fine essay on the novel.) Only feather-bedded ignorance could wax wroth and censorious over his 'gentility' and 'snobbishness'. Expectations have shaken but not rotted him. He suffers in a variety of very real ways, he does all he can for Magwitch, he knows shame, he pays. To make reparation, to pay, goes far towards releasing the victim from irony's toils, towards dissolving the irony. Pip ends with more than he could properly have expected, but no more than he has shown himself to deserve.

*

The victim of the cruellest irony can rise superior to it; and not solely because of our instinctive pity. In Thomas Mann's novella, *The Black Swan*, the widowed Rosalie von Tümmler is and always has been a lover of great, beneficent Nature. It has ceased to be with her, as with Abraham's wife Sarah, after the manner of women; but when she falls in love with a young American, her menstrual flow begins again. What she supposes a miracle of Nature has another explanation—an inoperable tumour. She has loved Nature, for a moment she had mistaken Nature, but now she accepts Nature with the old love and trust. To disguise death as resurrection, she tells her daughter just before the end, was not a lie but goodness and mercy.

Strange, perhaps, that it should be a male author who treats so female a matter with such impeccable delicacy and persuasiveness.

Frau Stöhr of *The Magic Mountain* is an ignorant, silly and malicious gossip, given to such verbal solecisms as 'cosmic' when 'cosmetic' is meant. On the death of the young captain Joachim, she demands between sobs that the *Erotica* should be played at the hero's grave. She is not all that far out. The atmosphere in the International Sanatorium Berghof is a febrile mixture of the heroic and the erotic, as love, short of time, battles it out with death. ('Is it my fault,' the director asks, 'that phthisis and concupiscence go together?') Joachim is a true hero, vowed to the soldier's life—his determination to lead it brings about his death, heroically, back in bed—but even so he is drawn against his will to Marusja, a pretty, full-bosomed fellow patient. (On whom

Hans Castorp, Joachim's cousin, passes the ghastly comment that chest trouble is the last thing one would accuse her of.) The victims here are victims of tuberculosis, not of irony. Even Frau Stöhr escapes death by irony through the aptness of her malapropism.

*

One of love's little ironies, you would say, when you read in *The Man Without Qualities* that 'Two weeks later Bonadea had already been his mistress for a fortnight.'

The original Bonadea, Musil intimates, was a goddess of chastity whose temple in ancient Rome became, by some strange turn in its fortunes, a centre of debauchery. Ulrich's new mistress, to whom he gives this nickname without her realizing why, is scientifically speaking a nymphomaniac, but the account we get of her, though by no means a glossing over, deters us from regarding her with repulsion, contempt or mockery. Apart from this little idiosyncrasy, she remains a good wife as well as a fond mother. Quiet and majestic, she is a high-minded woman, 'capable of uttering the words "the true, the good and the beautiful" as often and as naturally as someone else might say "Thursday" '.

Bonadea's ideal is a tranquil mode of life within the family circle, and her only fault is that

she was liable to be stimulated to a quite uncommon degree by the mere sight of men. She was by no means lustful; she was sensual in the way that other people have other troubles, such as sweating of the hands or blushing easily; it was apparently congenital, and she could never do anything about it.

Chained to her husband by some inner compulsion incomprehensible to her, 'she was unfaithful to him in order to escape from him, but while being so she talked about him, or the children that she had had by him, and at the most unsuitable moments'. We also gather that in between bouts of what the author terms 'weakness' she could be a considerable trial to her gentlemen friends:

she was full of the claims of respectability . . . One had to be truthful and good, to be sympathetic towards all misfortune, to be devoted to the Imperial House, to respect everything respected and in matters of morality to be as sensitive and gentle as at a sick-bed.

We don't need to blush for this nymphomaniac; we blush with her.

'God knows, war's a plain and tough job,' says the tubby little General Stumm, conscious of his lack of sophistication. 'But sex just happens to be the very territory where, as you might say, it goes against one's honour as an officer to let oneself be treated as a layman.' A simpler comic portrait but still not a simple figure of fun, the General conscientiously inspects the Imperial Library in pursuit of a great controlling idea for the forthcoming Imperial anniversary. Since there are three and a half million tomes there, he surely doesn't have to read every single one of them! His retort to that is, 'in warfare, too, one doesn't need to kill every single soldier, and yet every single one is necessary'.

Back to real life, and the eighteenth-century rationalist and reformer, Thomas Day, author of *The History of Sandford and Merton*. Animals were included in his programme of enlightenment, and he was killed while trying a new and humane way of training a colt. No cause for carollings there; we are aware of the irony as one of fate in its most caddish if not malevolent aspect: an incident for Hardy perhaps, albeit the kind of true story that writers of fiction steer well clear of. V. S. Pritchett's comment on it, untouched by knowingness or *schadenfreude*, goes some way to cheer us, as such glosses often can: 'The Age of Reason conceived wild nature and the noble savage to be tamer than they were.'*

*

The gentle side of irony's tongue is rarely noted by the experts,

---

*To restore the balance, there is the anecdote of the dog who saved his master's baby from a venomous snake. His master returned and, seeing the dog covered in blood and the cradle overturned, at once killed him. I have read that the dog was subsequently canonized as St Guinefort.

possibly because it is confused with the plainly irreconcilable tendency we call sentimentality. And similarly the intensity of longing at its heart. More generally thought of as a ruthless though necessary weapon deployed against futile hopes and foolish or injurious idealism, irony can evoke the forfeited (but never quite forgotten) ideal, regaining as it were a brief apprehension of lost paradise by sneaking in through the back gate of the garden, less well guarded than the main entrance. The ironist is not bound by intellectual honour to speak the one and immediate and present truth—though intellectual honour may seem, to the well-disposed, to be his sole motivation—but in what he implies or incidentally adumbrates he can, like Macduff, remember that such things were, or might have been, and even wonder for a moment whether they could yet be.

When, instead of working as an agent of dissolution, picking off false solaces and inflated ambitions, irony plays a part in unexpected reconciliation or restitution, we incline to call the result a fairy-tale. The embittered weaver, Silas Marner, thinks his stolen guineas have been mysteriously restored to him—and on New Year's Eve, when folklore has it that one's luck can turn—but his poor eyes deceive him. The heap of gold is the yellow-haired foundling, Eppie, who will release his soul from its 'cold narrow prison' and restore him to life.

Or if not a fairy-tale, then a 'Christmas story', as Michel Tournier describes his 'Mother Christmas'. The setting here is a village split by the traditional enmity between clerics and radicals, the Catholic school and the State school. This always comes to a head at Christmas, when Midnight Mass (at six in the evening of the 24th) and its living crèche clash with the head of the State school, dressed up as Father Christmas, distributing toys to his pupils.

On this occasion a new State teacher has recently arrived, a divorced woman with a three-months-old baby; obviously secular, yet she does go to church, and even lends her baby to the priest to be Little Lord Jesus. The usual confrontation takes place, except that the baby starts to howl as soon as the priest

157

ascends the pulpit. Its mother is sent for. But in comes Father Christmas in person, who picks up the baby, unbuttons his red robe, and offers an ample breast to Little Lord Jesus. Peace descends on all around.

Not that we are strongly tempted to read the story as an allegory, a promise of universal and permanent peace between Church and State. It is just a 'nice story', suitable for a short-lived season of good will. It takes a sterner irony—the deaths of Romeo and Juliet—to bring about something more modest, the end of a feud between two families.

Brecht's 'The Good Lord's Package—A Christmas Story' differs in that, while the irony involved is fairly sweet, there are victims; though since they are the intending persecutors, and have some excuse for their behaviour, and are let off lightly, this doesn't count for much. It is Christmas Eve in Chicago, in 1908. Some rancorous jokers give a man who obviously lives in fear of the law what they consider an appropriate present—pages from an old street directory listing nothing but the addresses of police stations. As he undoes the string his eyes fall on the scrap of newspaper wrapped round the present, and his face grows radiant. He has read there that the affair in which he was suspected has long ago been cleared up. The bitterness of the out-of-work jokers vanishes and they proceed to enjoy their modest Christmas. 'Amid the general satisfaction,' the narrator concludes, 'it was of course quite irrelevant that it was not we who had sought out that sheet of newsprint but God.'

'Sound natural feeling, say what you like, has no taste.' Tonio Kröger was talking about art, but art has a way of coinciding with life. And a modern Romeo and Juliet might have recourse to irony in a reconciliation scene of their own, following a lovers' tiff perhaps. Despite its reputation, irony allows us to declare ourselves—to convey, not the opposite of what we mean, but what we mean—where a sophisticated shyness or pride would inhibit plain speaking. (In life, as in art, the fear or *pudeur* relating to the expression of emotion isn't as unnatural or reprehensible as some rationalists make out.) In *Reflections on 'The*

158

Name of the Rose' (1985) Umberto Eco envisages the nice example of a cultivated young couple in slight difficulties. The man
cannot tell the woman 'I love you madly', because 'he knows that
she knows (and that she knows that he knows) that these words
have already been written by Barbara Cartland'. So he says
instead, 'As Barbara Cartland would put it, I love you madly.' In
an age of lost innocence—perhaps Adam and Eve were the last to
talk in such tones—you cannot speak innocently of love. 'Why
does almost everything seem to me like its own parody?' asked
the composer Leverkühn, another of Thomas Mann's characters. And yet you can still speak of love, thanks to 'the game of
irony'.

But how can less resourceful persons convey their love, those
who may well read Barbara Cartland with ingenuous enjoyment
but would never presume to express themselves as freely as her
characters do, those who lack the benefit of irony? Fortunately
they have other ways; and he too knows that she too knows (and
that she knows that he knows) that they love each other.

*

Even had I a talent for taxonomy I doubt if I should know in
which class to place an incident related in Barbara Trapido's
novel, *Brother of the More Famous Jack* (1982), an incident so
unlikely that it must have had a basis in fact. The heroine is
distressed after the death of her baby; or rather, she is 'disturbed', which has become a stronger adjective. She hears on the
radio the words, 'Now we have a humanist's despair before the
News', and tells herself that the radio announcer had plainly
addressed himself to her alone. Reason insists that this cannot
be—the words were 'Now we have a few minutes to spare before
the News'—but there is, she perceives, a comfort to be got out of
feeling that you are completely crazy. And there is, since being
crazy would mean that her baby was not really dead, she had only
imagined it. But she is not mad; she has heard something which
applied perfectly but was not actually spoken. The irony dwells in
what we might pompously term 'creative misunderstanding'; it

reflects no discredit on the woman, it points wryly to a human need.

Certainly no one is the victim of a notice, ingratiating and almost congenial, seen in an Oxford pub, for victimization would be bad for business: 'If the floor is covered with cigarette ends please use the ashtrays.' A lower class of customers is to be found, one supposes, in the City of London pub which declares, with a pleasing litotes, 'Don't ask for credit as a smack in the mouth sometimes offends.'

William Golding records the story of a clergyman congratulating a Wiltshire gardener on his success in clearing a patch of land: 'You have done well, my man, with God's help'; to which the gardener, who may never have heard of irony, replied: 'You should have seen this place, Vicar, when God had it to Hisself.' A reasonably amiable retort, nothing like a smack in the mouth, yet some of us may hope that the vicar—to whom, as it happened, the land belonged, if not God Himself too—felt a faint stinging sensation.

*

'Not to take yourself seriously is an affront to God,' writes Amiel: the tendentious verdict of an assiduous diarist, or a pious Christian. Others may view the self-ironist as a gentle altruist. A poem of Corbière's, called 'Ça?', has as epigraph: 'What? . . . (*Shakespeare*)'. A species of anti-manifesto or *ars poetica* in reverse, it ends: 'L'Art ne me connaît pas. Je ne connais pas l'Art.' The indicated locale—'Préfecture de police, 20 mai 1873'—suggests that the poem, which takes the form of question and answer, is self-exculpatory and self-explanatory rather than self-disparaging. In Laforgue's 'Dimanches' the speaker begins: 'I was about to give myself with a "I love you", when I realized, not without pain, that for a start I didn't really possess myself.' And he ends with a self-apostrophe: 'Come on, lowest of poets, always stuck indoors, you'll make yourself sick! . . . So go and buy yourself a couple of sous' worth of hellebore. It'll make a little outing for you.' Hellebore was believed to cure madness, and one species is used today in treating heart trouble. Laforgue's speaker has lost his girl; and when Corbière's hero, in 'Bonne Fortune et fortune', at last plucks up courage to brush against the girl he fancies in the street (Rue des Martyrs, according to the subscription), she smiles slyly, holds out her hand to him—and presents him with two sous.

We shouldn't feel too sorry for these self-ironizing poets, who 'stand, so to speak, with an unposted letter bearing the extra regulation fee before the too late box of the general post office of human life'. They are not Prince Hamlets, happily for them, nor were they meant to be, and out of their voluntary victimization they make their little songs. Rimbaud made a gay and engaging song in 'Ma Bohème'—*his* Bohemian life rather than the idealized version. But his coat at any rate was ideal, so threadbare as to be little more than the idea of a coat. A devotee of the Muse, what splendid amours he has dreamt of! His inn was under the stars, whose twinklings by some reasoned disordering of the senses evinced themselves as a gentle frou-frou. Sitting at the roadside, he strummed at the elastics attaching trouser-ends to ruined shoes as if playing a lyre, one foot held close to his heart.

We mustn't forget that notable victim, perhaps the worst sufferer of all: the ironical person him- or herself. Like Miss Wade of *Little Dorrit*, herself her own worst enemy, the ironist could say, 'I have the misfortune of not being a fool.' If Miss Wade could have been habitually imposed upon instead of habitually discerning the truth, she 'might have lived as smoothly as most fools do'. In addition to the bad reputation so easily acquired, there is the consequent sadness, for Kierkegaard remarks in his *Journals* that sadness means being alone in having understood something true and finding oneself in company with those who misunderstand. (There are of course sadder sadnesses.)

Arising from an obsessive tendency to relate everything to 'the idea' instead of letting one's mind amble along half-asleep, irony is a sort of paralysing debility which, 'as everyone knows', may prove fatal. Worse, Kierkegaard continues, 'Irony is an abnormal growth; like the abnormally enlarged liver of a

161

Strasbourg goose it ends by killing the individual.' From Goethe's little grain of salt we have moved to pâté de foie gras.

To close on a more delicate note . . . An interchange so gentle and so aptly professional that one wouldn't think of it as harbouring irony was reported recently in a Pakistani literary-academic journal. It seems that a 'respectful' (though possibly mischievous) university student, when asked by the attractive German teacher to form a simple sentence using two different personal pronouns, came up with: 'Madam, ich liebe Sie.' Amused, the teacher replied: 'If you really love me, why are you so formal? Just say, "ich liebe dich" .'

Conclusion

ALTHOUGH (or because) irony is notoriously a major literary mode or industry these days—it is thirty years since Northrop Frye found us 'in an ironic phase of literature'—and only popular literature (which we take to be non-literature) is, we are told, predominantly non-ironic, those intent on a career in writing are advised against admitting it except in the smallest and most discreet of doses. As noted, it confuses and repels readers, who sense some obscure threat to their peace of mind. In advance of their reacting, they have the feeling that whichever way they jump they will be jeered at by some invisible witness. It is just as well that Swift is not living at this hour, when in the aftermath of the death of God we are so much more sensitive about our pride than we used to be when we were immortal souls.

As for writing about irony, that too is risky since like enough you will emerge as either a smart alec or a dim-wit. Nevertheless, if you are an academic, publishing even on so equivocal a theme may help you to gain promotion. As we know, all teachers are good teachers, but in any structure involving seniority some need to be picked out as more good than others.

*

A world without irony would have to be either an earthly paradise, where it could never arise for there would be nothing to provoke it, or else an earthly hell, where it was never allowed to show its face. Our world seems unlikely ever to become an earthly paradise. Do men really seek peace and liberty, as they tell us? Not at all, according to Miguel de Unamuno: 'They look for peace in time of war—and for war in time of peace. They seek liberty under tyranny—and tyranny when they are free.' (Which suggests that we shouldn't be too quick to blame our governments, since they merely oblige.) On the other hand, the continued presence of irony must be a sign that neither is our world as yet an earthly hell.

Irony lives in the ample territory between those two extreme states; it acknowledges what must be, contends against what should not and need not be, and intimates what conceivably could be. On occasion as close as the pen can come to the sword, alternately anodyne and tonic, until nothing on earth can sustain us any longer it is a source of endurance and courage and even, in its oblique and tentative way, of hope. Another ambiguous gift, it may be, but a gift all the same.

*

A conclusion ought to take the shape, however inexplicit or shadowy, of 'and so we see'. It may happen, if infrequently, that an author comes to doubt the goodness of his subject. But it must be in some sense ironic should he end with less than total faith in the truth or even (the last attribute to be given up) the beauty of his

163

work. (Not, it has to be said, that much of the present book is my work, exactly.) But . . . Irony itself often ends with three dots. And at times begins its reverberations therewith.

REFERENCES

2 *unusual classifier*. William Empson; 'Let it go', *Collected Poems*, 1955.

Raymond Preston. Chaucer, 1952.

3 *Kierkegaard. The Concept of Irony*, 1841; tr. Lee M. Capel, 1966.

A Chaucerian scholar. Helen Cooper: *The Structure of The Canterbury Tales*, 1983.

4 *Rameau's Nephew*. Denis Diderot, 1762; tr. Jean Stewart and Jonathan Kemp, *Diderot, Interpreter of Nature*, ed. Jonathan Kemp, 1937.

5 *Samuel Johnson's. Dictionary of the English Language*, 1755.

7 *Erich Heller. The Ironic German: A Study of Thomas Mann*, 1958.

9 *Socrates*. For the passages cited, see Plato: *Euthyphro, Apology, Crito, Phaedo, Phaedrus*, tr. Harold North Fowler, 1914.

10 *Rilke's unicorn*. 'Das Einhorn', *Neue Gedichte*, 1907.

12 *Italo Svevo. Saggi e pagine sparse*, 1954; *Italo Svevo*, P. N. Furbank, 1965.

Nietzsche. 4 May 1889.

Friedrich Schlegel. Lyceumsfragmente, 1797.

14 *'Well – well'*. The three passages are from *Don Juan* (1819–24).

Goethe. 'Willst du ins Unendliche schreiten'.

'Love in a hut'. 'Lamia', 1820.

F. R. Leavis. Revaluation, 1936.

17 *'the Socratic dialogues'. Lyceumsfragmente*.

18 *Peter Firchow. Friedrich Schlegel's Lucinde and the Fragments*, 1971; from which the quotation is taken.

earlier English version. By Paul Bernard Thomas.

'Irony is duty'. See *Friedrich Schlegel: Literary Notebooks 1797–1801*, ed. Hans Eichner, 1957.

19 *Kierkegaard. The Journals of Søren Kierkegaard*, tr. Alexander Dru, 1938.

20 *The Magic Mountain*. Thomas Mann, 1924; tr. H. T. Lowe-Porter, 1928.

21 *Pascal's saying. Pensées*, 1670.

    'The Fate of Pleasure'. Beyond Culture, 1966.

22 *Wordsworth's resounding affirmation*. Preface to *Lyrical Ballads*, 1802.

24 *'From Mythology'. Zbigniew Herbert: Selected Poems*, 1968.

25 *'the little grain of salt'*. Quoted by Thomas Mann in *Die Kunst des Romans*, 1939.

    Henri Frédéric Amiel. Fragments d'un journal intime, 1884.

    Doctor Faustus. Thomas Mann, 1947; tr. H. T. Lowe-Porter, 1949.

    'What more beautiful gift'. An Umbrella from Piccadilly, 1980; tr. Ewald Osers, 1983.

26 *Charles Morice*. See introduction to *Tristan Corbière: Selections from Les Amours Jaunes*, tr. C. F. MacIntyre, 1954.

27 *Alfred Appel, Jr. The Annotated Lolita*, ed. Alfred Appel, Jr., 1970.

28 *Borges*. 'The Gifts', *Jorge Luis Borges: A Personal Anthology*, ed. Anthony Kerrigan, 1968.

29 *Cavafy's poem*. See *C. P. Cavafy: Collected Poems*, tr. Edmund Keeley and Philip Sherrard, 1975.

    Auden. 'Musée des Beaux Arts', *Collected Shorter Poems 1927–1957*, 1966.

30 *'I a heathen?'* Recorded by K. A. Varnhagen von Ense.

33 *as Goethe claimed. Sprüche in Prosa*, 1819.

35 *Shakespeare's tableau. Henry VI*, Part III (II. v).

37 *The Times*. 10 April 1985.

38 *'The Last Laugh'. Sunrise with Seamonsters*, 1985.

    Henry James's verdict. In the memoir, *The Middle Years*, 1917.

39 *Kingsley Amis*. 'Getting It Wrong', *The State of the Language*, ed. Leonard Michaels and Christopher Ricks, 1980.

    Montherlant. Les Célibataires, 1934.

41 *'Ballad of Abbreviations'. The Collected Poems of G. K. Chesterton*, 1932.

42 *said Donne*. Sermon, Easter Day 1622.

43 *Empson.* 'Marvell's Garden', *Some Versions of Pastoral*, 1935.

44 *'The true end of satire'.* 'To the Reader', *Absalom and Achitophel*, 1681–2.

Johnson. 'Dryden', *Lives of the Poets*, 1779.

48 *'I Remember, I Remember'. The Less Deceived*, 1955.

'Cub'. Ukulele Music, 1985.

50 *the Grampus's remark. Alice Through the Needle's Eye*, Gilbert Adair, 1984.

Erik Satie's crack. Notebook; see *The Banquet Years*, Roger Shattuck, 1959.

51 *Alethea Hayter. The Times Literary Supplement*, 9 August 1985.

a phrase from De Quincey. Confessions of an English Opium Eater, 1821.

De Quincey's pleasantry. On Murder Considered as One of the Fine Arts, Second Paper, 1839.

Dan Jacobson. 'Time of Arrival', *Time and Time Again*, 1985.

52 *New Statesman.* 5 November 1965.

53 *'never trust the artist'. Studies in Classic American Literature*, D. H. Lawrence, 1924.

when Byron wrote to Lady Melbourne. 2 February 1815.

Some four years later. 26 July 1819.

54 *'as what gods give must be'.* 'This Last Pain', *Collected Poems*, William Empson.

Lamb. 'A Dissertation upon Roast Pig', *Essays of Elia*, 1823.

Douglas Johnson. The Times Literary Supplement, 26 April 1985.

55 *Michael Frayn. Constructions*, 1974.

56 *Father Urban. Morte D'Urban*, J. F. Powers, 1962.

58 *'every idle word'.* St Matthew 12: 36.

'Never forget, gentlemen'. These Eighty Years, Vol. II, H. Solly, 1893.

The hymn. Mrs C. F. Alexander, *Hymns Ancient and Modern*.

59 *'The Church is divine'. The Lake*, 1905.

' "They" '. *Collected Poems 1908–56*, 1961.

60 *St Paul.* Romans 11: 33.

Luis Buñuel. My Last Breath, tr. Abigail Israel, 1984; title of chapter 15.

60 *Mérimée. Henri Beyle*, pamphlet, 1850.

The hymn of Cowper's. 'Light Shining out of Darkness', *Olney Hymns*, 1779.

61 *A. A. Cleary's emblematic poet.* Editorial, *Thames Poetry*, Vol. II no. 16, 1985.

one of Job's comforters. Job 5: 9.

Elias Canetti. The Human Province, tr. Joachim Neugroschel, 1978.

Emerson. Journals, 1836.

62 *Gibbon. The Decline and Fall of the Roman Empire*, 1776–88.

William Walsh's summary. R. K. Narayan: A Critical Appreciation, 1982.

63 *Conversation with the Abbé Barthélemy.* See *Diderot, Interpreter of Nature*, op. cit.

64 *Marlowe's Faustus. The Tragical History of Doctor Faustus*, written *c.* 1588.

65 *Goethe's Faust.* First Part and Second Part, written between 1773 and 1831.

75 *'Which I was born'.* 'Verses on the Death of Dr Swift', 1731.

Swift told Pope. In a letter, 29 September 1725.

His Modest Proposer. A Modest Proposal for Preventing the Children of Poor People in Ireland from Being a Burthen to their Parents or Country, and for Making Them Beneficial to the Publick, 1729.

76 *Leavis.* 'The Irony of Swift', *The Common Pursuit*, 1952.

77 *Christopher Hitchens. The Times Literary Supplement*, 21 September 1984.

'like a chaste whore'. Time, 14 September 1953.

De Quincey. 1854 postscript to *On Murder Considered as One of the Fine Arts.*

78 *Empson. Using Biography*, 1984.

80 *Clough. Amours de Voyage.*

'Funeral Rites'. North, 1975.

81 *'With no poetic ardours fir'd'.* 'On lying in the Earl of Rochester's Bed at Atterbury', 1739.

Johnson's terminology. 'Cowley', *Lives of the Poets.*

John Carey. The Sunday Times, 25 August 1985; reviewing Maynard Mack's *Alexander Pope: A Life.*

84 *'A Story which I Like'. Poems 1950–1974*, The Paradigm Press, 1984.

'Un Dîner en ville'. Les Plaisirs et les jours, 1896.

Gore Vidal. 'Some Memories of the Glorious Bird and an Earlier Self', *Matters of Fact and of Fiction*, 1977.

85 *'some mean, monstrous ironist'. The Dynasts*, Act VI, scene 5.

'the one bright book'. 'Why the Novel Matters', *Phoenix*, D. H. Lawrence, 1936.

86 *in a review. Cosmopolis: An International Review*, January 1896.

Virginia Woolf. Diary, Vol. 3, 25 July 1926.

94 *(The abysses . . .).* Henry James's response to Edith Wharton's confession that she had been rather disappointed by a reputedly 'unpleasant' novel; quoted by her in the introduction to the World's Classics edition (1936) of her novel, *The House of Mirth*.

96 *Remembrance of Things Past.* Quotations are taken from the translation by C. K. Scott Moncrieff and Terence Kilmartin, 1981.

97 *De l'amour.* 1822; *Love*, tr. Gilbert and Suzanne Sale, 1957.

98 *'Three Million Yen'.* Tr. Edward G. Seidensticker, *Death in Midsummer and Other Stories*, 1967.

99 *an early sketch.* 'Regrets et rêveries, VI', *Les Plaisirs et les jours*.

100 *Donne.* 'Lovers' Infiniteness'.

101 *Imlac's inconsistencies. Rasselas*, Samuel Johnson, 1759.

'In short measures'. 'To the Immortal Memory and Friendship of that noble pair, Sir Lucius Cary and Sir H. Morison', Ben Jonson.

102 *'Ah, but a man's reach'.* 'Andrea del Sarto', Robert Browning.

Matthew Arnold. 'Absence'.

The Psychopathology of Everyday Life. Tr. Alan Tyson, *The Standard Edition of the Complete Psychological Works of Sigmund Freud*, Vol. VI.

104 *Jokes and their Relation to the Unconscious.* Tr. James Strachey, as above, Vol. VIII.

Lichtenberg. See *The Lichtenberg Reader*, ed. and tr. Franz Mautner and Henry Hatfield, 1959.

109 *Josef Skvorecky's observation. The Engineer of Human Souls*, tr. Paul Wilson, 1985.

Gavin Ewart. 'Gods and Heroes', *The Young Pobble's Guide to his Toes*, 1985.

110 *'Now thank we all our God'.* Quotations come from *Bertolt Brecht:*

Poems 1913–1956, ed. John Willett and Ralph Manheim, 1976.

111 *'We are all brothers'.* Heine, letter of 6 November 1840.

112 *Martin Esslin's phrase.* 'Icon and Self-Portrait', *Encounter*, December 1977; actually in speaking of Brecht's dramatic theory.

'Here you have someone'. 'Of Poor B. B.'

the poem in question. 'The Solution'.

'great harvest-leader'. 'Die Erziehung der Hirse', ballad of 1950.

'meritorious murderer'. In a poem written in his last months, first published in West Germany in 1982; see 'Brecht's Stalin Poems', Martin Esslin, *Encounter*, February 1984.

114 *Shaw's bon mot.* 'The Rejected Statement', 1909; document submitted to the Select Committee on Stage Plays (Censorship).

115 *'three unspeakably precious things'. Following the Equator*, 1897; heading to chapter 20.

116 *Malcolm Bradbury's Dr Jochum. Stepping Westward*, 1965.

117 *Brigadier Adly el-Kosheiry. The Times*, 20 May 1985.

118–19 *'downright insulting'; 'join the debate'.* A letter in *The Times*, 23 August 1985.

119 *Günter Grass.* 'Kafka and his Executors', *On Writing and Politics 1967–1983*, 1985.

the finest thing. Amphitryon 38, 1929.

120 *Jaromír Hořec.* See *Back to Life: Poems from behind the Iron Curtain*, ed. Robert Conquest, 1958.

'even a black market'. Prisoners of Fear, Ella Lingens-Reiner, 1948; see *The Survivor*, Terrence Des Pres, 1976.

Karl Kraus's reflections. Die Dritte Walpurgisnacht; see 'Protective Custody', *In These Great Times: A Karl Kraus Reader*, ed. Harry Zohn, 1976, 1984.

121 *Books you were going to write. Ulysses*, James Joyce, 1922.

122 *Goethe.* Recorded by Friedrich Wilhelm Riemer.

'Expiation'. The Descent of Man and Other Stories, 1904.

Schlegel. Athenäumsfragmente, 1798.

Culture and Environment. F. R. Leavis and Denys Thompson, 1933.

Robert Giroux. Ninth Annual Richard Rogers Bowker Memorial Lecture, 1981.

123 *Evelyn Waugh. A Little Learning,* 1964.

Dorothea. Middlemarch, 1871-2.

D. H. Lawrence. Studies in Classic American Literature.

'Murke's Collected Silences'. The Stories of Heinrich Böll, tr. Leila Vennewitz, 1986.

Robert Musil's counter-irony. The Man Without Qualities, 1930-43; tr. Eithne Wilkins and Ernst Kaiser, 1953-60.

124 *George Eliot. Middlemarch.*

Nietzsche. Also Sprach Zarathustra, 1883-92.

'How to Tell a Major Poet'. Quo Vadimus?, 1939.

Orwell. 'As I Please', *Tribune,* 28 January 1944; *The Collected Essays, Journalism and Letters of George Orwell,* Vol. III, 1968.

'The Horse Marines'. A Diversity of Creatures, 1917.

Brecht. 'Little Epistle in which certain Inconsistencies are remotely touched on', *Bertolt Brecht: Poems 1913-1956,* op. cit.

Marianne Moore. 'Poetry', *Collected Poems,* 1951.

(Auden). 'In Memory of W. B. Yeats', *Collected Shorter Poems, 1927-1957.*

Macaulay. 'Milton', 1825; *Critical and Historical Essays Contributed to the Edinburgh Review,* 1843.

Alex Comfort. 'Sublimation', *Haste to the Wedding,* 1962.

story. See Byron's note to alternative concluding couplet of stanza 11, 'Dedication', *Don Juan,* where he seeks to excuse himself for rhyming 'Laureate' and 'Iscariot'.

Boileau. 'Satire II', 1664.

125 *Huck Finn's book. The Adventures of Huckleberry Finn,* Mark Twain, 1885.

Tonio Kröger. 'Tonio Kröger', 1903; *Stories of a Lifetime,* Vol. I, Thomas Mann, 1961.

126 *Karl Kraus's yearnings.* 'The Beaver Coat', *In These Great Times,* op. cit.

Voltaire. Dictionnaire philosophique, 1764.

Céleste and Marie. Remembrance of Things Past (Cities of the Plain).

127 *'sensible warm motion'. Measure for Measure* (III. i).

128 *Rochester.* 'A Satire Against Mankind', *c.*1675.

171

128 *'If I can't be famous'. After Martial*, Peter Porter, 1972.

Duchess of Malfi. The Duchess of Malfi, John Webster, c.1613.

both bane and boon, to lack . . . is wound. 'Behold this little Bane', Emily Dickinson, c.1878, *The Poems of Emily Dickinson*, 1955.

'the bright foreigner'. Emerson, *Journals*, 1849.

129 *Dick Swiveller. The Old Curiosity Shop*, Dickens, 1841.

Yeats. 'A Prayer for my Daughter', *Michael Robartes and the Dancer*, 1921.

'this is the monstruosity in love'. Troilus and Cressida (III. ii).

130 *Stendhal. De l'amour.*

131 *one of the sketches.* 'Regrets et rêveries, VI'.

Mme de Breyves. 'Mélancolique villégiature de Madame de Breyves'.

132 *'Many waters'.* Song of Solomon.

The Revenger's Tragedy. 1607.

'Futility'. 1918.

133 *Sir Epicure Mammon. The Alchemist*, Ben Jonson, 1610.

medieval story. See *The Charms of Love*, Edward S. Gifford, 1962.

Mr Mercaptan. Antic Hay, Aldous Huxley, 1923.

Professor Heller. 'Man ashamed', *In the Age of Prose*, 1984.

Allan Rodway. English Comedy, 1975.

135 *Jonson.* 'On My First Son', *Epigrams*, 1616.

136 *'anxious for to shine'. Patience*, W. S. Gilbert, 1881.

'coarse irony'. 'Über die Unverständlichkeit'.

what elsewhere he adduced. Ideen; see *Friedrich Schlegel: Literary Notebooks 1797–1801*, op. cit.

Byron. Don Juan.

137 *H. L. Mencken. Minority Report*, 1956.

138 *Deputy Culture Minister.* Roger Boyes, *The Times*, 9 September 1985.

Kraus's saying. Beim Wort genommen, ed. Heinrich Fischer, 1955; and see *Half-Truths & One-and-a-Half Truths: Selected Aphorisms of Karl Kraus*, ed. and tr. Harry Zohn, 1976, 1986.

Sidney Hook. See 'A Recollection of Bertolt Brecht', *The New Leader*, 10 October 1960.

138 *Philip Howard. Weasel Words*, 1978.

139 *Nicholas Bagnall. A Defence of Clichés*, 1985.

Frank Gonzalez-Crussi. Notes of an Anatomist, 1985.

140 *The War of the Worlds.* H. G. Wells, 1898.

Senator Buddenbrook. Buddenbrooks, Thomas Mann, 1901.

Jonathan Wild. The Life of Mr Jonathan Wild the Great, 1743.

Volpone. Ben Jonson, 1606.

Chauntecleer. The Nun's Priest's Tale.

142 *'Theory and Teaching'. Critical Theory and the Teaching of Literature*, Vol. 3 of Proceedings of the Northeastern University Center for Literary Studies, ed. Stuart Peterfreund, 1985.

'An irony has no point'. 'Double Plots', *Some Versions of Pastoral.*

'Streets'. New York Review of Books, 13 August 1970.

144 *V. S. Pritchett's definition.* 'Henry Fielding', *A Man of Letters*, 1985.

145 *'most wrecked and longest'.* 'China', William Empson, *Collected Poems.*

146 *'Then he will crown'.* 'On the Birth of his Son', tr. Arthur Waley, *170 Chinese Poems*, 1962.

147 *the report. China's Sorrow*, Lynn Pan, 1985.

150 *Sheridan. Life of Sheridan*, Thomas Moore, 1825.

Herbert Read. See *Recollections*, Geoffrey Grigson, 1984.

Victor Wulpy. 'What Kind of Day Did You Have?', *Him with His Foot in His Mouth, and Other Stories*, Saul Bellow, 1984.

151 *Andrew Young's crab.* 'The Dead Crab', *Complete Poems*, 1974.

153 *Q. D. Leavis's fine essay. Dickens the Novelist*, F. R. and Q. D. Leavis, 1970.

156 *V. S. Pritchett's comment.* 'Thomas Day', *A Man of Letters.*

157 *Silas Marner. Silas Marner*, George Eliot, 1861.

'Mother Christmas'. The Fetishist and Other Stories, 1983.

158 *'The Good Lord's Package'. Bertolt Brecht: Short Stories 1921–1946*, ed. John Willett and Ralph Manheim, 1983.

159 *Leverkühn. Doctor Faustus.*

160 *William Golding.* 'Wiltshire', *A Moving Target*, 1982.

160 *Amiel. Fragments d'un journal intime*, 19 November 1854.

161 *'stand, so to speak'. Ulysses.*

162 *Pakistani literary-academic journal. The Journal of the English Literary Club*, Session 1983–4, University of Peshawar.

Northrop Frye. Anatomy of Criticism, 1957.

163 *Miguel de Unamuno. The Tragic Sense of Life*, 1913; tr. Anthony Kerrigan, 1972.

INDEX

Acton, Harold, 84
Adair, Gilbert, 50
Alexander, C.F., 58
Amiel, Henri Frédéric, 25, 160
Amis, Kingsley, 39
Appel Jr., Alfred, 27
Arendt, Hannah, 108
Arnold, Matthew, 102
Auden, W.H., 29, 124
Austen, Jane, 83-4, 141, 142, 151

Bagnall, Nicholas, 139
Ballard, J.G., 139
Barnes, Julian, 26, 55
Beaumarchais, Pierre Augustin Caron de, 115-16
Beethoven, Ludwig van, 136
Bellow, Saul, 150
Blake, William, 38
Boileau, Nicolas, 124
Böll, Heinrich, 25, 113, 123
Booth, Wayne C., 1-2, 37, 51, 61
Borges, Jorge Luis, 28
Bradbury, Malcolm, 116
Brahm, Alcanter de, 37
Brandes, Georg, 12
Brecht, Bertolt, 110-13, 124, 138, 158
Browning, Robert, 102
Buckingham, George Villiers, 2nd Duke of, 44
Buckinghamshire, John Sheffield, Duke of, 133
Buñuel, Luis, 60
Burgess, Anthony, 57
Butler, Samuel, 61-2
Byron, George Gordon, Lord, 13-14, 15-16, 46, 53, 66, 118, 136

Caesar, Julius, 136
Canetti, Elias, 61
Carey, John, 81
Carlyle, Thomas, 13
Carroll, Lewis, 13, 27
Cartland, Barbara, 159
Cavafy, C.P., 29, 111
Charles II, 45
Chaucer, Geoffrey, 2, 3, 140-1
Chénier, André, 121
Chesterton, G.K., 41
Cleary, A.A., 61
Closs, August, 17
Clough, Arthur Hugh, 45-7, 80
Coleridge, Samuel Taylor, 13, 32
Comfort, Alex, 124-5
Confucius, 148
Conrad, Joseph, 21, 109, 152-3
Conrad, Peter, 13
Cooper, Helen, 3
Corbière, Tristan, 26, 160-1
Corelli, Marie, 37
Cowper, William, 60

Day, Thomas, 156
De Quincey, Thomas, 51, 77
Dickens, Charles, 37, 129, 153-4, 161
Dickinson, Emily, 128
Diderot, Denis, 4, 63
Donne, John, 42, 43, 100
Douglas, Lord Alfred, 30
Dryden, John, 12, 44-5, 85
Dundy, Elaine, 22
Dyson, A.E., 1

Eco, Umberto, 144, 158-9
Eliot, George, 123, 124, 157

Eliot, T.S., 6, 27, 117
Elizabeth I, 107
El-Kosheiry, Adly, 117
Emerson, Ralph Waldo, 61, 128
Empson, William, 2, 5–6, 43, 78–9, 142–3, 145
Essex, Robert Devereux, Earl of, 107
Esslin, Martin, 112
Esther, Book of, 31
Ewart, Gavin, 109

Fielding, Henry, 77–9, 140
Firchow, Peter, 18
Flaubert, Gustave, 84–5, 141–2
Fleming, Sir Alexander, 54
Fowler, H.W. and F.G., 37
France, Anatole, 60
Franz Josef I, 137
Frayn, Michael, 55
Freud, Sigmund, 102–6
Frye, Northrop, 162
Fuller, Roy, 109
Furst, Lilian R., 15–17, 141

Gallimard, Editions, 117
Genesis, Book of, 58
Gibbon, Edward, 62
Gilbert, W.S., 136
Giraudoux, Jean, 119
Giroux, Robert, 122
Glicksberg, Charles I., 8
Goering, Hermann, 137
Goethe, Johann Wolfgang von, 14, 25, 30, 33, 46, 65–7, 68, 72, 122, 129, 150, 162
Golding, William, 160
Gonzalez-Crussi, Frank, 139–40
Gosse, Edmund, 86
Grass, Günter, 82, 119
Guiccioli, Countess Teresa, 53
Guillotin, Joseph Ignace, 31

Hardy, Thomas, 29, 60, 85–7, 147, 156
Harington, Sir John, 107–8
Hayter, Alethea, 51
Heaney, Seamus, 80
Hegel, Georg Wilhelm Friedrich, 8, 21
Heine, Heinrich, 104, 111–12, 114, 120

Heller, Erich, 7, 133
Heller, Joseph, 60–1, 123
Hemmings, F.W. J., 52–3
Herbert, Zbigniew, 24–5
Hitchens, Christopher, 77
Hitler, Adolf, 110
Hodgson, Ralph, 140
Hook, Sidney, 138
Hŏrec, Jaromír, 120
Howard, Philip, 138–9
Huxley, Aldous, 133

Inge, William, 116
Issa, Kobayashi, 134–5

Jacobson, Dan, 51–2
Jagger, Mick, 37–8
James, Henry, 38, 84, 88–95, 109, 115, 141
Job, Book of, 61
John, St, 42, 56, 58
John XXIII, Pope (Baldassare Cossa), 62
Johnson, Douglas, 54–5
Johnson, Samuel, 5, 15, 38, 44, 81, 101
Johst, Hanns, 137
Jonson, Ben, 101, 124, 133, 135, 140
Joyce, James, 27, 119, 121–2, 161

Kafka, Franz, 119
Keats, John, 13, 14–15
Kierkegaard, Søren, 3, 8–10, 18, 19, 57, 150, 151, 161–2
Kipling, Rudyard, 124
Kraus, Karl, 120, 126, 138, 150

Laforgue, Jules, 160–1
Lamb, Charles, 54
Lao-tzu, 146
Larkin, Philip, 48
Laurence, St, 144
Lautréamont, Comte de, 41
Lawrence, D.H., 53, 123
Leavis, F.R., 14–15, 76
Leavis, Q.D., 153
Leigh, Augusta, 53
Lenin, Vladimir Ilich, 111, 113
Lichtenberg, Georg Christoph, 104

Index

Li Po, 146
Lodge, David, 54–5
Louis XVI, 116
Luke, St, 56, 57

Macaulay, Thomas Babington, Lord, 124
Magritte, René, 41
Mahathir, Mohamad, 116
Mahler, Gustav, 27
Mahood, M.M., 69
Mann, Heinrich, 17, 93
Mann, Thomas, 17, 20, 25, 26, 64, 93, 94, 125–6, 130, 137, 140, 154–5, 158, 159
Mao Zedong, 111
Marlowe, Christopher, 64–5, 68
Martial, 118, 128
Martin, St, 78
Marvell, Andrew, 42–3
Matthew, St, 24, 56, 58, 99, 128
Maupassant, Guy de, 141
Melbourne, Lady, 53
Mellor, Anne K., 13–14
Melville, Herman, 123
Mencken, H.L., 137
Mérimée, Prosper, 60
Milbanke, Annabella (Lady Byron), 53
Milosz, Czeslaw, 20–1, 23–4, 25, 123
Milton, John, 43, 114–15
Mishima, Yukio, 98
Molière, 32, 121
Montherlant, Henry de, 39
Moore, George, 59
Moore, Marianne, 124
Morice, Charles, 26
Muecke, D.C., 1–2, 12–13, 26–7, 37, 50, 86, 134, 137
Muggeridge, Malcolm, 77
Mullen, Peter, 58
Musil, Robert, 123, 125, 137, 155–6
Musset, Alfred de, 121

Nabokov, Vladimir, 27
Napoleon I, 60
Narayan, R.K., 62–3
Nero, Emperor, 29, 130

Nietzsche, Friedrich, 12, 58, 124, 150
Nixon, Richard, 41

Ortega y Gasset, José, 25
Orwell, George, 124
Owen, Wilfred, 132

Parnell, Charles Stewart, 57
Pascal, Blaise, 10–11, 21
Pasternak, Boris, 117
Paul, St, 60, 61
Perelman, S.J., 38
Po Chü-i, 146
Polanski, Roman, 147
Pope, Alexander, 12, 75, 80–2
Porter, Peter, 128
Powers, J.F., 56
Preston, Raymond, 2–3
Prior, Matthew, 130
Pritchett, V.S., 144, 156
Proust, Marcel, 84, 96–102, 126, 131–2
Purcell, Victor, 135–6

Quinault, Philippe, 124

Rabelais, François, 53–4
Racine, Jean, 130
Ravel, Maurice, 27
Read, Herbert, 150
Reading, Peter, 48–50
Reed, T.J., 129
Ricks, Christopher, 142–3
Rilke, Rainer Maria, 10
Rimbaud, Arthur, 161
Rochester, John Wilmot, Earl of, 81, 128, 133
Rodway, Allan, 133–4
Rossini, Gioacchino, 12
Rousseau, Jean-Baptiste, 104
Russell, Jeffrey Burton, 59–60

Sarit, Thanarat, 40
Sassoon, Siegfried, 59
Satie, Erik, 29, 50–1
Schlegel, Friedrich, 12, 15, 16, 17–19, 65, 122, 136, 150
Schopenhauer, Arthur, 12
Seifert, Jaroslav, 25

Shaftesbury, Anthony Ashley Cooper, 1st Earl of, 44, 45
Shakespeare, William, 5-6, 30, 35, 68-74, 90, 104, 107, 117, 127, 129, 134-5, 157
Shaw, George Bernard, 114, 115
Shelley, Percy Bysshe, 140
Sheridan, Richard Brinsley, 38, 150
Skvorecky, Josef, 109
Socrates, 9-10
Song of Solomon, 132
Southcott, Joanna, 86
Spender, Stephen, 52
Spiegl, Fritz, 41
Stalin, Joseph, 111, 112, 113, 138
Steele, Sir Richard, 38-9
Steinach, Eugen, 128
Stendhal, 60, 97, 115, 129, 130-1
Stephen, St, 57
Sterne, Laurence, 18, 36, 145
Stewart, Mary, 52-3
Stravinsky, Igor, 29
Su Tung-p'o, 146
Svevo, Italo, 12
Swift, Jonathan, 11, 17, 59, 63, 75-7, 137, 162

Tennyson, Alfred, Lord, 38
Theroux, Paul, 38
Thompson, Dunstan, 84-5
Tourneur, Cyril, 132
Tournier, Michel, 157-8
Trapido, Barbara, 159-60

Trilling, Lionel, 21-3
Turner, F. McD. C., 114, 143
Twain, Mark, 115-16, 125

Unamuno, Miguel de, 163

Valéry, Paul, 117
Vidal, Gore, 84
Villon, François, 118
Virgil, 124
Voltaire, 60, 104, 126

Wagner, Richard, 12
Walsh, William (1663-1708), 28
Walsh, William, 62
Waugh, Evelyn, 123
Webster, John, 128
Wells, H.G., 140
Werfel, Franz, 74
West, Nathanael, 78
Wharton, Edith, 122
Whately, Richard, 58
White, E.B., 124
White, Hayden, 25
Wilde, Alan, 4, 5
Wilde, Oscar, 30, 55
Williams, Nigel, 123
Wilson, Angus, 30
Woolf, Virginia, 86
Wordsworth, William, 22, 23

Yeats, W.B., 57, 129
Young, Andrew, 151